TO L...

FROM

W. M.

STORIES OF
Encouragement
AND FAITH IN
Life Challenging
TIMES

PASTOR W.M. HARRIS

WESTBOW
PRESS®
A DIVISION OF THOMAS NELSON
& ZONDERVAN

WestBow Press books may be ordered through booksellers or by contacting:

WestBow Press
A Division of Thomas Nelson & Zondervan
1663 Liberty Drive
Bloomington, IN 47403
www.westbowpress.com
1 (866) 928-1240

ISBN: 978-1-9736-4744-7 (sc)
ISBN: 978-1-9736-4743-0 (hc)
ISBN: 978-1-9736-4745-4 (e)

Library of Congress Control Number: 2018914270

Print information available on the last page.

WestBow Press rev. date: 12/13/2018

Stories of Encouragement and Faith in Life Challenging Times.

This book is dedicated to my mother, Minnie Lee Harris, Hollins and Will Hollins the man I called Daddy Will, who raised me from the age of five years old until I got married and moved into my own home. My humble and sincere appreciation to them for bringing me out of the cotton fields of Mississippi, in hopes of a better way of life for me. I regret all the times that I made my mother cry, due to my bad choices. I am so thankful that she dedicated me to the Lord, and I appreciate the fact that she never gave up on me and never stopped praying for me. I remember her encouraging me to seek the Lord for my life, I am who I am today because my mother's prayers moved the hand of God in my life.

If the true stories that are in this book, can give encouragement to just one individual to open their heart and mind to the possibilities and the potential that God has placed within them, my journey will not have been in vain.

Encouraged to make room in your heart

LUKE CHAPTER 2:7 (NKJV) SAYS," And she brought forth her firstborn son, and wrapped him in swaddling clothes, and laid him in a manger, because there was no room for them in the inn". There was no room in the inn for Joseph, Mary, and Jesus; and so, they stayed in a stable. Then Jesus was wrapped in swaddling clothes, which were long strips of cloth used to wrap infants; and he was placed in a manger. A manger is the feeding trough for livestock, which in this case was filled with hay and doubled as a cradle.

The fact that there was no room in the inn can be seen to symbolize that sinful mankind has no place for Jesus Christ in their lives. The very God of the universe was not welcome on earth! How sad it is that our lives are so full of unnecessary clutter that we do not have room in our lives for the very God who created us. As I look at the condition of the world, the broken families, homes, lives, and children, I see such a need for the Savior to come into our lives and do a new thing that will revolutionize our thinking and living.

We make room in our lives for things that make no sense, add no value, and bring no lasting joy to our situations. Yet, we refuse to allow the Prince of peace, the king of kings, and the Lord of lords into our lives that can bring a change to our mind, heart, and spirit. King David had filled his heart with sinful lust and even murder, but he asked God to create within him a clean heart and renew within him a clean spirit and God did because David made room in his heart for God.

I realize that everyone is not a Christian, but I also understand that if I have something or know of a tool or a technique that can change one's life I should be willing to share that with whoever is in need and whosoever will listen. My job is to tell others what I've come through and the experience that has changed my life, and my way of living. Peering into the broken homes and lives of inner-city families, I see the hopelessness, frustration, and despair that chokes the very life out of the families that are living in a sea of poverty and violence.

Young men that walk the streets of the city with no job, no education, and no life skills to prepare them for a productive future. They carry $600 smart phones and they text people instead of talking to them; and in their home, they have 50-inch Smart TV's that is equipped with the latest X box and every gaming device that is available. They walk around in $200 Jordan gym shoes and apparel, and their lives are filled with baby mama drama.

Young women walking around looking for love in all the wrong places, hoping to find value and love in some young man's heart; thinking that if she gives him a child he will love her even more. We all make room in our lives for unnecessary pain, failure, and disappointments; rather than for life, love, and fulfillment of purpose. There is a story in the Bible about a demon possessed man that was healed when he made room in his heart for Jesus Christ.

Luke 8:27-37 says," (NKJV) And when he stepped out on the boat on to the shore there he met a certain man from the city who had demons for long time, and he wore no clothing and he did not live in a house but in the tombs. When he saw Jesus, he cried out and felled down before him and with a loud voice he said," what have I to do with you, Jesus son of the highest God?

I beg you, do not torment me! For he had commanded the unclean spirit to come out of the man for it had often seized him, that he was kept under guard, bound with chains and shackles; and he broke the bonds and was driven by the demon into the wilderness. Jesus asked him, what is your name? And he said Legion," because many demons had entered him. And they begged him that he would not command them to go out into the abyss.

Now a herd of swine was feeding there own the mountain. So, they begged him that he would permit them to enter the swine, and he permitted them. Then the demons went out of the man and entered the swine, and the herd ran violently down the steep place into the lake and drown. When those who fed, them saw what had happened, they ran and told it in the city and in the country.

Then they went out to see what had happened, and came to Jesus, and found the man from whom the demons had departed, sitting at the feet of Jesus, clothed and in his right mind. When we make room for Jesus in our hearts, mind, and spirit, we also can be unchained, unshackled, and set free. There are many people in this world that is in the same situation as this demon possessed man, who was under guard, bound with chains and shackles.

Demonic possession and oppression by the powers of darkness always results in people being bound and shackled spiritually. In our present day, people have filled their lives with addiction, lust, anger, violence, pride, fear, doubt, perversion, the occult, and so much more, and they are bound just as this man was. Jesus set this man free through the power of the spirit. That same Holy Ghost Spirit is available to set us free today and break every chain that binds us.

Pastor W.M. Harris

But you my friend, must make room in your heart for the only one that can change your life and the lives of those you love. Will you make room today in your heart? Remember, there is power to break every chain, to break every chain that binds you or your love ones. Friends. Be encouraged.

Voices of encouragement

I REMEMBER AS A KID in Mississippi when I got my first bicycle, I didn't know how to ride it and I fell from it too many times to remember. After so many times of falling, my father said to me," stop looking at your feet as you paddled," and look at him." It was very hard to do, but he kept saying," look at me, you can do it, "look at me.

One day as I was learning to ride my new bike, I took my eyes off my father and his instructions, and I begin to watch my feet as I paddled my new bike. The next thing I remember, I had run under a large piece of farm equipment and banged my head pretty good. All because I took my eyes off my father and his instructions, who was encouraging me to look at him and not at my feet. I did painfully learn the lesson which my father taught me that day, which was to pay attention to where I was going and to follow instructions.

Dr. Tony Evans relates a story in his book of illustrations about Keri Strug, the Olympic gymnasts. In the 1996 Olympics, Keri Strug had the weight of the Olympic gold medal for her team on her shoulder shoulders. All she had to do was have a successful vault, and the United States would get the gold. There was one problem. When she did her first vault, she sprained her ankle, as she could barely walk. She fell; she did not get the score she needed for the U.S. team to win.

As she sat there on the mat with tears falling down her face, she cried for two reasons. One, she was in pain. And two, there was no way she could make the score to win the victory in this situation. But she had another jump. She had another vault. She got up. She felt like giving up, but her coach stood on the sidelines and said, "You can do it, Keri. You can do it, Keri. I believe in you. You can do it." As she limped to get ready to try to do a vault, she could barely move.

She told an interviewer, after the vault, that all she could do to keep going was keep her eyes on the coach. He kept her from focusing on her ankle. This girl was really hurting. She was crying. But she had an encourager who believe in her. She found strength from his encouragement that she didn't have. Even with the limp, she took off running, and did her flip on the vault. She had to nail the landing to win. She had to try to do this with an ankle that was injured. With her coach's encouragement holding her up, she conquered her impossibility.

She earned a high enough score for the U.S. team to win the gold - all because of her coach's encouragement. Encouragement changes your performance. Just a little bit of encouragement can take you a mighty long way, that's why it's so important for us to encourage one another. Encouragement should be a daily activity in our home, in the lives of our family members, in the lives of those around us, and in the lives of those that we encounter daily.

When the disciples saw Jesus doing what was seemingly impossible by walking on the water they were afraid. Matt 15:27 (NKJV) "Peter said," Lord, if it is you, command me to come to you on the water." So, Jesus said come." And when Peter had come down out of the boat, he walked on the water to go to Jesus." Peter had just accomplished the impossible, he walked on the water at Jesus command and he kept his eyes focused on Jesus. Everything was going great for Peter, if his focus was on Jesus.

Everything changed the moment Peter took his eyes off Jesus and began to focus on his circumstances and situation. Matt 14:30 (NKJV) says," But when Peter saw that the wind was boisterous, he was afraid; and beginning to sink, he cried, saying, "Lord, save me." And immediately Jesus stretched out his hand, and caught him, and said to him, O thou of little faith, wherefore did thou doubt?

Jesus did the physically impossible, and he calls us to walk along beside him and do likewise. He told us in his word, John 14:12 (NKJV) "greater things then this shall you do". If we reject our fears and choose to trust Christ, he will bring about the miraculous in our lives also. Be encouraged my friends and listen to the voice of other encouragers around you.

Encouragement to seek the Lord

THERE WAS A TIME IN my early years when I thought I didn't need any help from anyone. I thought I was big enough, strong enough, and tough enough to handle any problems that came my way. Instead of functioning out of reality and truth, I was functioning out of my emotions which were leading me astray and down a path of destruction. I remember one situation of growing up as a child in Chicago's inner-city, and functioning out of my emotions as a gang member. I felt like a big shot, I felt protected and safe, I felt that there were no dangers because my gang had my back.

As I functioned out of my emotions, I convinced myself that there were no dangers. Then I began to see the ugly truth behind my gang involvement, I saw shootings, and Molotov cocktails thrown at rival gang members houses. I suffered the humiliation of being chased from school by rival gang members and being shot at. Had I continued to function out of my emotions instead of reality, I would have died in my emotions; but thank God, I had a praying mother that encouraged me early in my life to seek the Lord.

Dr. Tony Evans relates this story from his book of instructions. One day while flying his plane, a pilot noticed a small cloud up ahead. He decided to just fly through it. Once he got amid the cloud, he realized that it wasn't as small as he had thought. He decided to pull up and out of it but after pulling up for a lengthy period, he decided to try to point the nose of the plane down to get out of this cloud. Still not able to come out of the cloud, the pilot began to get a little disoriented. With all his maneuvering, he began to wonder if he was right side up or upside down.

Sweat began pouring down his face, because he did know his position in the cloud. He started to feel upside down. He checked his instruments and they said the plane was still right side up. He felt like the plane had tipped over, but the instruments said the opposite. The pilot made the decision to believe the instruments even though his emotions were leading him differently. It took all his energy to believe that those instruments were telling him the truth. Finally, he came out of the cloud, not far from the ground, because the cloud was low.

When he came out, he was right side up. Had he believed what he felt. He would have been a dead man; but he acted on what the instruments said, even though he felt differently. While many times our emotions and feelings will lead us into disaster, the word of God is an instrument that gives solid guidance and directions we can count on. Had I continued to function in my emotions and followed what I felt, I too would've met an early demise. Our emotions and feelings can lead us to destruction, but if we are encouraged to follow the Lord and his word we will find guidance and direction that will lead us to safety.

In second Chronicles, the people depended upon King Hezekiah to make the right decisions and lead them out of harm's way. He gathered the people together in the open square of the city and gave them encouragement. In Chapter 32:7-8 (NKJV) he said to the people," be strong and courageous; do not be afraid or dismayed before the king of Assyria, nor before all the multitude that is with him; for there are more with us than with him. "With him is an arm of flesh, but with us is the Lord our God, to help us and to fight our battles." And the people were strengthened by the words of Hezekiah king of Judah.

Had King Hezekiah functioned out of his emotions, the king of Assyria would have defeated and destroyed King Hezekiah, his people, and his city. But King Hezekiah encouraged his people to seek the Lord, he said to them," with the king of Assyria is an arm of flesh; but with us is the Lord our God, to help us and to fight our battles." The people were strengthened by the words of King Hezekiah of Judah. When we function out of our emotions, we function out of our feelings and those feelings are not always based upon evidence.

King Hezekiah had seen the evidence of the Lord who is mighty in battle, and he encouraged the people to seek the Lord to fight their battles. My friends, I encourage you today to seek first the kingdom of God, and his righteousness, and all these things shall be added unto you. Be encouraged.

Encouraged to be strong and courageous

HAVE YOU EVER FELT THAT there is a greater purpose for your life than that which you are currently living? But fear and doubt stood in the way as self-made mountains that you and other doubters willingly erected in your life. You hear the call and feel the urge, but still you convince yourself to stay in a safe place where average is the norm. Your dreams cry out to you and gasp for air, as a small flame that is being extinguished under a wet blanket. You feel the urgency to act, but you are paralyzed with fear because you don't know how to be strong and courageous in the battle to keep your dreams alive.

I remember when I left my home and my family in Chicago to follow my dreams. It was a very uncertain time in my life, and I was both anxious and excited at the same time. Yet, I fixed my eyes on the journey that life was beckoning me to follow, because I felt that if I didn't leave Chicago I would die there before my time. I left everything that I knew and the way of life that I was familiar with, to follow the unknown. I felt something pulling at me that I had no control over, but I knew that I had to follow that desire.

I had come to a fork in the road, and now I had to decide which direction to go with my life. I could stay with the familiar path of family, friends, predictable situations, and a scripted life. Or, I could choose to pursue the dreams that was placed deep down in my sub-conscious mind. I chose to follow my dreams, although I didn't know where they were taking me because the path was so unclear and uncertain. Yet, the urge to follow this impulse was so great that I couldn't resist its magnetism.

As this great urge tugged at my very soul, I became even more restless because I knew there was more to my life than what I saw with my nature eyes. I didn't have a clue of where I was going or how to get there, but I knew I had to make this journey. Sometimes God wants to grow us in a way that takes us to a faith stretching place beyond the limits of our imagination and move us to the other side of fear where we can follow his purpose for our lives.

In the Book of Joshua chapter 1, Moses had just died, and God called Joshua to lead the people. God told Joshua in Chapter 1:2 (NKJV)" Moses my servant is dead. Now therefore, arise, you and go over this Jordan, you and all this people, to the land which I am giving to them, the children of Israel. God also said to Joshua, 1:5-9 (NKJV)" No man shall be able to stand against you all the days of your life: as I was with Moses, so shall I be with you: I will not fail you, nor forsake you.

Be strong and of a good courage: for to this people you shalt divide for an inheritance the land, which I swore unto their fathers to give them. Only be thou strong and very courageous, that thou may observe to do according to all the law which Moses my servant commanded you: do not turn from it to the right hand or to the left, that you may prosper wherever you go. This book of the law shall not depart from your mouth; but you shalt meditate in it day and night, that you may observe to do according to all that is written in it. For then you shalt make thy way prosperous, and then you shalt have good success." I believe God brought Joshua to a faith stretching place, to move him pass his fear and doubt. God called Joshua and encouraged him to be strong and very courageous, because no man would be able to stand against him all the days of his life.

God gave Joshua a personal promise to encourage him to be strong and very courageous. What an ego boost, to have the God of Heaven personally assure you of your success and to back it up with," I will not fail you, nor forsake you. As I prepared to make my own journey, I was reminded of God's words to Joshua to be strong and very courageous; because I knew that God was the same yesterday, today, and forever. I also knew that if God be for you, who can be against you?

God gave Joshua the formula for success when he told Joshua," 1:8 (NKJV) This book of the law shall not depart out of your mouth; but you shalt meditate in it day and night, that you may observe to do according to all that is written in it: for then you shalt make your way prosperous, and then you shalt have good success. Be encouraged my friends, God has given you the same promise that he gave Joshua through his Son Jesus Christ, we too can be strong and courageous through Christ to follow our dreams.

Encouraged to Remember

I WAS READING MY BIBLE a couple days ago, when I began to remember how good God is and how he guarded me, guided me, delivered me, and provided for me. I remembered how he kept me safe from hurt, harm, and danger. I remember how he opened the doors of opportunity for me that was closed, and how he made a way when I could see no way. I remember one time when I was going through financial difficulties, and there have been many times. I remember how God would have people come up to me and give me what was called a," Pentecostal handshake.

A Pentecostal handshake is when someone walks up to you and shakes your hand, but they have money in their hand and it goes into your hand during the handshake. God caused my friends to bless me as well as my enemies, even when my enemies though they were destroying me God caused them to build me up and bless me. I remember one situation when I wrote a play and a skit about slavery and the plight of African-Americans during the Jim Crow era. I had a live slave auction, where slaves were being auctioned off to the highest bidder.

I wanted to show the students of the school where I worked, a live portrait of the perils that the African-American people faced during that time. I even had signs over both water fountains which said," whites only, and colored only." One of the teachers became upset about my presentation and called the newspaper and a local television station, hoping to turn my presentation and skits into an exaggerated fact that did not expose the ugliness and hatred that racism and prejudice produces when left unchecked.

The teacher meant it all for evil, but the mighty hand of the God turned it around for my good. The newspaper people and photographers took pictures of the live slave auction, and they interviewed me and asked why did I write the skits and do the presentation? I told them," I wanted the students to see and understand the atrocities that the African-American people had to endure during these tough times. When the TV station anchor person interviewed me, I was asked the same question.

My answer was the same, the television anchor person said," it was a wonderful thing that I was doing, and schools should teach more about African-American history." The writeups and pictures in the newspaper were fantastic, and in the background of the slave auction photo, the students are seen with their eyes open wide in amazement at the sight of such a spectacle.

I remember that it was the mighty hand of God that turned these situations around in my favor. God wants us to remember that his hand is strong, and mighty to save. In the book of Joshua, 4:21-23 (NKJV) says," Then he spoke to the children of Israel, saying: "When your children ask their fathers in the time to come, saying, what are these stones? Then you should let your children know, saying, Israel crossed over this Jordan on dry land.

For the Lord, your God dried up the waters of the Jordan before you until you had crossed over, as the Lord your God did to the Red Sea, which he dried up before us until we had crossed over. That all the people of the earth may know the hand of the Lord, that it is mighty, that you may fear the Lord your God forever." God wanted Joshua to build a monument from 12 stones to be a visible reminder to coming generations of the power of God.

God does not want the reality of his mighty and delivering power to be forgotten from one generation to another. It is not enough to talk about the great revivals of the past. God wants every new generation to know the hand of the Lord, that it is mighty. God wants every individual and every church in every generation to call upon him for a fresh visitation of his spirit and presence.

In Jeremiah 33:3, (NKJV) "God's people are told to call to God so that he will show them great and mighty things. God is trying to teach his people that he isn't playing games. He is the God of the past, the present, and the now. My friends, be encouraged and remember that the hand of the Lord is mighty.

Encouraged to be the Change

I HEARD A STORY ONCE about a pilot, a computer expert, a preacher, and a Boy Scout. They were all aboard a small airplane when it developed engine trouble with smoke and fire rushed from the engine, it was then that the pilot announced that the plane was going to crash and there are only three parachutes on the plane.

The pilot said, "I need a parachute because I have three small children and a young wife at home that needs me, he took a parachute and jumped out of the plane." The computer expert said," I need a parachute because I have all this knowledge that the world cannot live without, so he immediately grabbed a parachute and jumped out of the plane."

The old preacher looked at the Boy Scout and said," son, God has been good to me, I have lived a long life and have been many places and done many things, so you take the last parachute and jump, and I will go down with the plane. The Boy Scout looked up at the old preacher and said," Mr. preacher Pastor Sir, that computer expert didn't take the time to read, and he grabbed my school backpack and jumped out of the plane.

That old preacher was a perfect example for the young Boy Scout to see what sacrificing self for others is truly all about. We also must be the difference that we want to see in other people lives, many people can talk a good game, but truth is not found in talking about it, the truth is seen in the application of the task.

We must be the difference that we tell our young people to be, our duty is to show them how to live and how to treat others. Most of the young people that I encounter today have no idea of respect, integrity, or honor for themselves, their peers, or their elders. Most of the youth today are being despised because they have not been taught how to be the difference that the world need.

First Timothy Chapter 4:12 (NKJV) says," let no one despise your youth, but be an example to the believers in word, in conduct, in love, in faith, in purity." Does this sound like most of the generation of youth that you know and are affiliated with? If so, when do we begin to make a difference in the lives of these young people through teaching and discipline, if not now, when? If not here, where? If not us, who?

God wants to use young men and women as he uses older ones, young people should never look down on themselves just because they are young. God wants to use people, both young and old, to reach our world for Jesus Christ; and a young person's energy and enthusiasm is a valuable gift, God has given young people the power to change the world. They should let their imaginations soar, step out on faith, and let God do great things through them.

We need to show them how important they are, and the potential that lies dormant deep within them waiting for such a time as this. The Bible says in Proverbs Chapter 22:6 (NKJV)," Train up a child in the way he should go, and when he is old he will not depart from it."

There are so many young people who wait for their turn to serve because you and I are getting older and we need young people to be ready to take a leadership role in society. They will either learn the right way by loving caring individuals with the child's best interest at heart, or they will learn the wrong way by individuals with malice and wrong motives. You, my friend, have the power to be the change in someone's life, choose wisely. Until next time be encouraged my friends.

{Call to action tools}

Prayer

All mighty God, I pray that the eyes of my heart would be open to your will and your purpose for my life. I pray that you would use me to be an example for those that come after me and that my life would be used as a teaching tool to train up the next generation to walk in your truth.

Be the example.

1Timothy 4:12 (NKJV), Let no one despise your youth, but set the believers an example in speech and conduct, in love, in faith, in purity.

Set the example.

To act in a way that others want to copy, particularly by doing something noteworthy. We must set the example for the younger men and women to follow.

Train up.

Proverb 22:6 (NJKV) Train up a child in the way he should go, and when he is old he will not depart from it.

When you train someone up, you teach them new skills and you give them the necessary preparation to reach the standard required for a job or activity.

Encouraged to know that God provides

HAVE YOU EVER PRAYED FOR something that you wanted, and God gave you so more than you could have ever imagined? Have you ever been in a storm that should have destroyed you and everything you possessed, but God's hand of mercy shielded you from its destruction? Have you ever had a problem that was too big for you to handle, but God said," don't worry I got this? Have you ever been in a situation that was designed for evil toward you, but God turned it around for your good? Have you ever had to fight a giant that could crush you, but God gave you the victory over it?

I don't know about you, but those events are frequent occurrences in my life, yet I realized that I couldn't defeat the enemies of my soul on my own. Nor do I have power over the unpredictable circumstances that invade my life quite often. I have come to know that God is my strength and my refuge, my source that creates every resource that is available to me, my peace in the storm, and I am ever so thankful for His love and protection.

I am reminded of a devastating storm that came through Mississippi when I was a child, it was one of the worst storms that I can remember. My mother and I were sitting alone in the back room of our small home as this storm raged all around us. The storm seemed as though it was right on top of us, the thunder was so loud that it literally shook the walls of the tiny house we lived in. As the thunder rumbled overhead, I remember hearing my mother praying to God as I sat on her lap terrified, but the faith and confidence that I saw on my mother's face that night still reminds me today that God hears and answers the prayers of His children.

My mother was so confident that the God she served would answer her prayers, that we both fell asleep and slept through the remainder of that terrible storm. After the storm had passed, I remember waking up to hear my mother praying and thanking God repeatedly for protecting us. Thanking God for bringing us through such a storm that uprooted trees out of the ground, and down powerlines all around us.

I saw the mighty hand of God moved by my mother's unwavering prayers, and I have also learned to pray and be thankful for the many storms that the Lord has brought me through. There has also been seasons of uncertainties, and doubt that I had to walk through, agonizing moments of fear that left me broken and battered, but through it all I am so thankful that God kept me safe in his arms. There have even been times when I questioned God, and said," where are you Lord? I am in the valley of despair Lord, but, where are you? This burden is too heavy for me to carry Lord, where's to strength that you promised? Then I remember, it was only in the quietness of my soul that I heard Him speak and say," here I am, fear not, be of good courage, for I will not leave you nor forsake you. Once again, I begin to thank Him for His faithfulness, even when I doubted and lost faith, He remained faithful and true. I'm reminded of Psalm 100:1-5 (NKJV) that says," Make a joyful shout unto the Lord, all ye lands!

Serve the Lord with gladness; come before his presence with singing. Know that the Lord He is God; it is He that has made us, and not we ourselves; we are his people and the sheep of his pasture. Enter into His gates with thanksgiving, and into his courts with praise: be thankful to him and bless his name. For the Lord is good; His mercy is everlasting; and his truth endures to all generations." Be encouraged my brothers and sisters, He is the faithful master that never sleeps, and he watches over his children ever so carefully. Let us be thankful and know that he is God our protector.

Encouraged to know that you are not alone

I AM SURE YOU HAVE heard or read Margaret Rose Powers," Footprints in the Sand. "The words bring such clarity to the phrase," Never alone." The message in her writing is that even when she though she was alone, God was still there in a way that she never realized before. In like manner, sometimes God must speak to our heart and our situation to let us know that we are not alone. In the book of Joshua 1:9 (NKJV) says," do not be afraid, nor dismayed, for the Lord your God is with you wherever you go."

These words spoke to the heart of Joshua and he was encouraged by the Lord God. When the Lord called Joshua to lead the people into battle for the promised land, Joshua was understandably afraid; but the Lord reminded him, "Do not be afraid, nor be dismayed, for the Lord your God is with you." Joshua chose to believe and obey the promise of God, and he embarked on an astounding 25-year adventure. He saw the river waters part, walls crumble, the sun stands still, and 31 kingdoms conquered, just to mention a few! Joshua depended upon God's power and gave him the glory for every victory.

He found that real courage is trusting in God, full maturity in surrendering to God, wise leadership in following God, and true obedience is out of a heart of love for God. The Lord still looks to do great things through servants with hearts like Joshua's. Do you find yourself alone and afraid sometimes, with your children and grandchildren all grown and gone out in the world to start their own lives? Does the condition of the world and the plight of the people cause you to fear for your safety?

Does the rise in healthcare and prescription drugs, economics, global warming, the loss of friends, family and loved ones, and of course your own mortality cause you to be afraid? Remember the paragraph in Margaret Rose Powers poem," during the most troublesome time in her life there was only one set of footprints. There have been so many times in my own life, when I could not see or feel the presence of God walking with me. 2 Cor 5:7 (NKJV) says," We walk by faith, not by sight." I have learned to trust in God, because He is God and not a man that He should lie.

Do you remember the Lord's reply? He assured her that He loved her, and that He is not a God that would abandon His children in their time of need. It is so calming and assuring to know that during our times of doubt and suffering, we are being carry through these situations in his strength and not our own. 1st Peter 5:7 (NKJV) says," Cast your cares upon Him, for He cares for you. This is a promise from God, and my mother taught me that I could always stand on the promises of God.

When my mother passed away at age 44, when my son passed away at age 19, when my great grandson passed away at age 2, when the doctor gave me the bad news that I had cancer, and when my wife left me, it felt like I was alone but I was not because he carried me during those times which were the lowest points in my life. Were there ever times in your life when you felt like everyone had abandoned you? God carried me through my lowest points, and he will carry you through yours also.

In the book of Joshua 1:2 (NKJV)," God tells Joshua Moses' assistant that his servant Moses is dead and that he will lead the people over the river Jordan, as I was with Moses, so I will be with you. I will not leave you nor for sake you. There have been leaders and trailblazers in your life, that mentored you, corrected you, and showed you the right way to live.

Maybe they have gone on to be with the Lord, and now it's your turn to step up and be the leader and trailblazer for your family. You must be strong and of good courage and be not afraid of the battles that lie ahead of you. We do not know what tomorrow holds, but we do know who holds tomorrow in the palm of His hand. When the night gets the darkness, and the day gets the longest, when your strength is depleted, and you stand facing the storms of life, you must remember you are not alone.

There is one who stands beside you who commands the wind, He holds back the rain, He shelters you from the storm; He says peace be still and the storm must obey. He whispers gently and lovingly into your spirit," I love you and I will never, leave you nor forsake you." Be encouraged my friends, God loves you and He is standing and waiting with open arms.

Encouraged to be the leader

HAVE WE FAILED OUR YOUNG men and women? Have we led them to believe that there is no hope for their future? Have we caused them to have no regard for life or the laws of this land? Have we caused them to live recklessly, to disregard life and act irresponsibly? Have we caused them to cast their moral conscience so far away that it is irretrievable? Is the condition of our young people our fault (the parents) or theirs (society)?

I would like to say that it is ours fault, parents, grandparents, people who say they love these children. After all, the apple doesn't fall too far from the tree, we who care for them and provide for them and teaching them right from wrong, or should I say, that they are right and everyone else is wrong. Teaching them to respect others, or should I say, to have no respect for others, remembering my child is a mini- me, so what I put in I get out.

We have been instructed to direct our children in the right way, you know, to train up a child; but in some cases, the train has run off the track. I ask you," when did we let go of the wheel? Who's driving the train? Is it someone with a learner's permit, or someone with an invalid operator's license? Or is it someone with a need for speed that was high on all the wrong things, and unable to see the danger signs and the warning lights?

Have we closed our eyes to the problems that we have created? While we try to shift the blame to others for the fire in our homes that we allow to burn out of control, and out of control it is. More prisons are being built, more homes are fatherless; more laws are being written to take away parental rights. More drugs are entering our neighborhoods, more young men and women are being lost in the system, and more young women are having babies at an alarming rate.

Matt 15:14 (NKJV) says," If the blind leads the blind, then they both fall into a ditch." If no one is willing to lead our young people, then who will they follow? The parent is the child's first teacher, that parent is leading in a positive or negative way even if they say nothing. I read a poem once that was quoted by John Maxwell, it was called "The Little Chap Who Follows Me," A careful man I want to be, A little fellow follows me; I do not dare go astray, for fear he'll go the self- same way." The main message is that the little chap is following him, watching him and doing whatever he sees him do. Our children are following in our footsteps, and the problem is that we went the wrong way and now they are going the wrong way also.

It's time to redirect our steps and correct our mistakes, it's time for men to come back home, not just to an address but to God's morals and values, to families, church and community. Whether we realize it or not, we are leading our children, even in our absence we are leading them. 89% of what a child learns comes through visual stimulation, 10% through audible stimulation, and 1% through other senses. So, it makes sense that the more children see and hear their parents being consistent in actions and words, the greater their consistency and loyalty. What they hear, they understand; and what they see, they believe, and somewhere between finding ourselves, we lost ourselves.

Billy Graham said," If we lose money, we lose nothing; if we lose health, we lose something, but if we lose character and integrity, we lose everything." I say to you my friend, you have greatness inside of you; your children have the same stuff within them. But someone must show them how to access it, you are the chosen one and you must show them the way. Be encouraged, be strong, be bold for your family, and take the lead, lead on.

Encouraged to break every chain

IT'S BEEN OVER 20 YEARS since I stopped smoking cigarettes, and I have never felt better in my life. As the world becomes more health conscious, I see people struggling with this addiction now more than ever. Not only nicotine addiction, but also drugs and alcohol are plaguing our homes, our families, and our lives. According to the American Cancer Society about 42 million people (somewhat fewer than 1 in 5) adults currently smoke cigarettes.

Tobacco use does not end with cigarettes: other forms of tobacco use are common. In 2013, a survey by the US: Substance Abuse and Mental Health Administration reported that 13.4 million people smoked cigars, and 2.5 million people smoked tobacco in pipes. The same survey reported 9 million people use smokeless or spit tobacco.

Tobacco use, including smoking cigarettes, cigars, e- cigarettes, and hookahs, (a hookah is an Oriental tobacco pipe with a long, flexible tube that draws the smoke through water contained in a bowl), as well as using chew or spit tobacco such as snus and snuff, is common among American youth, according to the most recent government surveys.

Despite declines in recent years, and 2012 nearly 1 in 4 male high school students (23%) and nearly 1 in 5 female high school students (18%) were found to be current users of some type of tobacco. Nearly

1 in 7 students (14%) were considered current cigarette smokers. Typically, about half of the students reported that they've tried to quit smoking during the past year. Cigar smoking was also common among high school students, (about 8% of females and 17% of males).

Even though flavorings are no longer allowed in cigarettes, "little cigars" (which often look like brown cigarettes) are sold in candy fruit flavors that appeal to youth. Also, in 2012, about 7% of middle school students use some form of tobacco, with cigarettes (nearly 4%) being the most common. Almost 3% had smoke cigars. In both middle school and high school, tobacco use was higher among male students for all products.

Behavioral problems have also been linked to smoking. Studies have shown that students who smoke are also more likely to use other drugs, get in fights, carry weapons, try to kill themselves, and take part in risky sex. According to the (NCADD), National Council on Alcoholism and Drug Dependence Inc. more than half of all adults have a family history of alcoholism or problem drinking, and more than 7 million children live in a household where at least one parent is dependent on or has abused alcohol.

Alcohol abuse and alcoholism can affect all aspects of a person's life. Long term alcohol use can cause serious health complications, can damage emotional stability, finances, career, and impact one's family, friends and community. Our children and family members, and our community do not have to suffer in vain. There is help.

There is power to break every chain, every bondage, every addiction, every problem, every circumstance, every hopeless situation, every life that is in disarray, every shattered dream, every home that is in shambles, there is power to break every chain that holds you in bondage. My mother showed me where the power was, and how to access that power.

But like most young people I was hardheaded, and I almost destroyed my life before I realized that I had to make a choice. In the book of Joshua 24:15 (NKJV),' Joshua says to the people, "And if it seems evil to you to serve the Lord, choose for yourself this day whom you will serve, whether the gods which your fathers served that were on the other side of the river, or the gods of the Amorites, in whose land you dwell. But as for me and my house, we will serve the Lord."

Joshua knew and remembered the victories he had won through the power of the Lord. Like Joshua I want my children and my family to be successful, not afraid, not living in bondage to any situation. So, it is my duty to teach them what has been taught to me, and to show them that there is a power that can break every chain, even the bondage of fear. Second Timothy 1:7 (NKJV) says," for God has not given us the spirit of fear; but of power, and of love, and of a sound mind. There is power to break every chain, the power lies in the name of Jesus Christ our Lord and Savior. Be encouraged.

Encouraged to build on a solid foundation.

THE HOUSE ON THE ROCK is a tourist attraction located between the cities of Dodgeville and Spring Green, Wisconsin. Opened in 1959, it is a complex of architecturally unique rooms, streets, gardens, and shops designed by Alex Jordan, Jr. The house on the rock is a fascinating place, and you must see it to believe it. How on earth this artist could conceive such a plan and bring it to life is beyond me, but I believe it is the perfect example to use with what I'm about to tell you.

As I read Matthew 7:24-28 (NKJV) I see why Jesus used such an analogy. Verses 24 and 25 says," therefore whoever hears these sayings of mine, and does them, I will liken him to a wise man who built his house on the rock. And the rain descended, the floods came, and the winds blew and beat on that house; and it did not fall, for it was founded on a rock. The house on the rock was designed in 1959, and it has stood for 57 years.

During that 57 years' hundreds of storms have beat up on that house, and yet it continues to stand because it was built on a rock. How many storms have your house been through, and is it still standing strong and unscathed. Let's talk about real storms in our lives that are meant to test our foundation, like dealing with the difficult or broken relationships. Going through a fiscal crisis, withstanding legal problems, unpleasant or painful health problems, the death of someone you love.

Dealing with rebellious children, facing something that brought public disgrace, being laid off from work, or dealing with drug or alcohol problems. The storms of life will come, but if the house is built up on a rock no matter what the problems are the house will stand. That rock is Jesus Christ, and no matter what storm comes your way, you will be able to withstand any storm because your house is built upon the rock.

I remember the storms in Mississippi that would cause my father to leave my mother and I in the house alone while he ran and hid under the bridge from the storm. While he hid from the storm under the bridge, my mother and I hid away from the storm in Jesus arms. My mother would call me to her side and we would set in this big rocking chair in the back room, and my mother would rock and pray with me in her lap all throughout the storm until it was over.

Sometimes the thunder would seem so loud, that I thought it was in the same room with us. I never understood why my father ran and left us alone, nor why he was so afraid of storms. But it was one thing that I did know, that Jesus Christ was the rock that my mother builds her house up on. He can bring peace in the mist of any storm that I will ever go through.

Currently uncertainty is around every corner, but one thing is certain, Jesus said I will never leave you nor forsake you. In him we stand and whether any storm. Verse 26 and 27 says," but anyone who hears these sayings of mine, and does not do them, will be like a foolish man who built his house on the sand: and the rain descended, the floods came, and the winds blew and beat on that house; and it fell. And great was its fall."

Look at the number of families that have fallen and been destroyed by divorce, fatherlessness, violence, alcohol and drug abuse. Our young people are committing suicide through cyber bullying, negative thinking, and no foundation to build on. Some people seem to have it all in life, money, power and fame; but still their lives come crashing down. Only Jesus Christ and the reality of God's word offers complete security in this world.

People who build their lives on anything other than this solid foundation will find that when the winds of change come, as they often do in life, their lives fall apart. For example, if we build our lives on anything that can be taken from us like our looks and popularity, first string on the varsity squad, a relationship, money, or a job then we will be insecure. An individual can only get so many face lifts, no matter how popular you are someone is going to dislike you for whatever reason. Praise God that Christ cannot be taken from us, nor can we be snatched out of his hand, nor will he ever leave us or forsake us!

That is true personal security. Friends, whatever storms that are raging in your life at this time did not come to stay, they came to pass. If your house is built upon the rock, you have a solid foundation that cannot be shaken by the storms of life. So, let the rains come, and the winds blow, and let them beat up on that house: but it will not fall, because it was built upon the rock, Jesus Christ. Until next time, be encouraged.

Encouraged to be thankful

COUNT YOUR MANY BLESSINGS, NAME them one by one, count your many blessings and see what God has done. Have you ever actually counted your many blessings? As I look back over my life and consider all the times that God has blessed me, and did so many wonderful things in my life, I must say thank you Lord.I realize that I have so much to be thankful for, I could've been dead, I could've been in prison, I could've been strung out on drugs, I could've been homeless, I could've been living in poverty, I could be without a job, I could've been born with a birth defect, and the list could go on and on.

So now I choose to stop and reflect over my life and say thank you, for all that you brought me through. Growing up in the mean streets of Chicago with gangs, drugs and violence on all sides of me, put me in danger of losing my life every day. I could've have been in the middle of a gang war and got shot up, but he protected me. I thank God that he protected me in my youth and kept me out of harm's way, in all my foolishness and stinking thinking he shielded me from the blast.

I choose to look back over my life with an attitude of gratitude, because Pastor Harris was not always the person that you see and know now. I am grateful for His strength, because I know of my weaknesses. I am grateful for the peace that's in my life now, because I know the storms that he brought me through. I am grateful for the valleys in my life, because I remember the mountains that he brought me over. I am grateful for the sunshine in my life, because I remember the dark days that he brought me out of.

I am thankful for the food that he gives me, because I remember many days being hungry. I am thankful for the joy that I now have in my life, because I remember the sorrow and pain that life inflicted upon me. I am thankful for the friends and family He placed around me, because I remember the agony of being so lonely. I am thankful that he did not condemn me for my sins, because I remember being guilty of everyone. I am thankful that he did not give me a spirit of fear, but he gave me power, love, and a sound mind.

Psalm 95:2 (NJKV) says," Let us come before His presence with thanksgiving." Thanksgiving, todah (toh-dah): the word "thanksgiving" means far more than just sitting down to eat a turkey dinner. Thanksgiving is a powerful spiritual principle. The Psalmist wrote: "Let us come before God's presence with thanksgiving." When we give thanks to God, we are both honoring and worshiping Him as God. God delights in hearing our Thanksgiving in the same way an earthly father is pleased to hear his own children expressions of gratitude for his goodness to them.

I read a quote the other day on thankfulness, "it said each day I am thankful for the nights that turned into mornings, friends that turned into family, dreams that turned into reality, and likes that turned into love. Here are some quotes on thankfulness that I have read and found heartwarming. Be thankful for what you have; you'll end up having more. If you concentrate on what you don't have, you will never, ever have enough" — Oprah Winfrey

Whatever happens in your life, no matter how troubling things might seem, do not enter the neighborhood of despair.

Even when all doors remain closed, God will open a new path only for you. Be thankful!"

— Elif Shafak, The Forty Rules of Love "Perhaps it takes a purer faith to praise God for unrealized blessings than for those we once enjoyed or those we enjoy now." — A.W. Tozer

"Those blessings are sweetest that are won with prayer and worn with thanks."

— Thomas Goodwin

We would worry less if we praised more. Thanksgiving is the enemy of discontent and dissatisfaction."

— H.A. Ironside

What a true statement that H.A. Ironsides just quoted," we would worry less if we praised more. Friends we have so much to praise God for, and to thank him for all that he is doing in our lives. Would you take the challenge? Count your many blessings, name them one by one, count your many blessings, and see what God has done. Sometimes we can get so bogged down in day to day activities, and we become so busy that we forget the lesson that was learned in elementary school.

Stop, look, and listen. Take time to look at where you are in life, remember where you've come from, and take time to say thank you for never leaving me alone.

When in doubt read Margaret Rose powers," Footprints in the Sand." Because sometimes God needs to remind us of what he said," I will never leave you nor forsake you." To that my friend, you can say thank you and live a thanks full life.

Until next time, be encouraged.

Encouraged to read
the instructions

I BOUGHT A VERY NICE chair from a thrift store some months ago, it was black with white leather stitching and it looked brand-new. I saw other people looking at the chair, so I immediately purchased it and took it home. I proudly set it in my computer room, but to my amazement when I sat in the chair it did not perform properly. I was so disappointed, I had this beautiful chair, but it did not work correctly.

It was a swivel chair that was supposed to lean backward, but instead of it leaning backward it would only lean forward. I was very disappointed, but at least I had a very nice chair sitting in the computer room. Now I have two chairs sitting in the computer room, both are swivel chairs and one works properly, and one doesn't. It became so irritating to sit in the chair, although it's very comfortable and looks good; but it only leans forward and when you attempt to get up out of it the chair leans forward and you slide downward.

I tried to turn the knob in the back of it, I tried to adjust it by the handle on the side of it and nothing worked. So, I gave up on the chair, and I said to myself now I know why the previous owner gave it away. The chair sat in our computer room, I really hated sitting in it because it didn't work correctly. One day a friend came over to work on my computer, and he said that's a nice chair; I said yes, it is but it doesn't work properly.

He said what you mean it doesn't work properly? I explained to him the problems I was having with the chair. He examined the chair and said whoever assembled the chair assembled it backward. That's why it's not working properly. I said you have got to be kidding me, is that why it's not functioning properly? The chair sat in the computer room for another two weeks, I got out of bed one night at 2 o'clock in the morning because I could not sleep, and I went and sat at the kitchen table and I began to pray.

I remember feeling very frustrated, because it seemed to me that I was not accomplishing my goals, my dreams or my vision that I believed God had given me for my life. I began to read the first chapter of Psalms, and it said, "God inhabits the praises of his people." So, I just began to praise God out loud, walking through my house just praising God out loud. As I walked in and out of every room praising God, I was led into my computer room and I begin to tell God that I need to turn my life around.

Then I remembered the chair, and how it needed to be turned around before it could function the way that it was meant to function. I was still praying and praising God as I rolled the chair into the kitchen so that I could work on it, just as the chair needed to be turned around to function properly, God said to me," so did you." As I turned the chair upside down to work on it, I saw the instructions on the bottom of it.

The previous owners did not read the instructions, because it clearly stated how the hardware was to be positioned on the bottom of the chair for it to work properly. Then I realized that I had not been following instructions that are clearly stated in my Bible, for my life to function properly. Then I began to see clearly why our lives are in such shambles and chaos, because we have not followed clearly stated instructions.

The instructions are there, and we choose to ignore them, because we can do it ourselves. I remember assembling a bicycle, but I had some spare parts left over and I thought they had sent extra parts. Had I read the instructions there would not have been extra parts left over, who needs instructions right? I was in the same situation as the chair was, I was in need of repair also, our young people are in the same situation, in need of repair, the families are in the same situation in need of repair. We need to turn our lives around, we are not functioning properly; we are not performing at our maximum potential.

I then went to get my tools to turn the hardware around on the bottom of the chair. Then I saw that I needed a special kind of tool to take the hardware off and turn it around the proper way in order that the chair could function properly. Again, I knew that I needed something out of the ordinary to turn my life around. So, does our youth, our families, and society also. Fortunately, I had access to the right tools to make the proper adjustments and now the chair functions properly.

We also have access to the only one that can change our lives, our youth and our families. But we must be willing to follow his instructions, seek first the kingdom of God, and his righteousness and all these things shall be added unto you. Are you ready to turn your children life around? Are you ready to turn your life around? Be encouraged and read the instructions.

Encouraged to have a heart transplant

IN THE BOOK OF EZEKIEL Chapter 36:27 (NJKV) it says," I will give you a new heart and put a new spirit within you; I will take the heart of stone out of your flesh and give you a heart of flesh." I heard a story some time ago about a black crow and a white dove who were best friends, they went everyplace together, and they did everything together; mostly bad but they were inseparable.

They were associated and recognized not because of their different color, but because of the same evil intent and thoughts in their heart. After the death of the black crow and although the dove was as white as snow, all everyone else recognized about him was the black evil heart inside of him. The moral of the story is, you may not be known by the color of your skin, but you will be known by the contents of your heart. Lately I have found myself with a harden heart toward certain people, and I know that's wrong of me, but some people just tend to rub you the wrong way; you know what I mean right.

I cannot be held responsible for the way that someone else acts toward me, but I am responsible for the way that I act toward another person. Because I oversee the words that come out of my mouth, and

I oversee the actions that I take toward another person. So therefore, I must guard my heart and my mouth. As I look at the political arena I see that it reflects the attitude of most of the world, and if this is the attitude of our would-be leaders then maybe those that follow them are of the same persuasion.

Everyone has a difference of opinion on every subject, but just because we do not agree on a matter does not mean that we must assassinate their character. Our words have power in them, therefore we must be very careful of what we say to other people and to ourselves. Our words are like a hammer that drives a nail into the wall, you can remove the nail from the wall, but the hole remains. We say hurtful words and then say we're sorry, we take back what was said but the pain of our words is still there.

Luke chapter 6:45 (NJKV) says," a good man out of the good treasure of his heart brings forth good; and an evil man out of the evil treasure of his heart brings forth evil. For out of the abundance of the heart his mouth speaks." I found it so necessary and comforting to read Ezekiel 36:27 (NJK) that said," I will give you a new heart and put a new spirit within you; I will take the heart of stone out of your flesh and give you a heart of flesh."

I even see the heart of stone in some of our children, a rebellious and angry spirit that leads them further into darkness and ambiguity. The question was asked of Fat Joe the rapper, why are our children so angry? His response was," everyone wants to be hard." I heard someone say," whatever is in the well, will come up in the bucket. In relationship to your heart, whatever is in the deep part of your heart will come to the surface when you speak and act.

An evil man out of the evil treasure of his heart brings forth evil, when you get angry does the evil man show up and bring evil treasure out of his heart or does the good man show up and bring good treasures out of his heart? Whatever man shows up first (good or evil) dictates the outcome of the matter, can you afford to say the wrong words at the wrong time? I don't know about you, but I must guard my heart always, because sometimes evil thoughts will try to creep in and take root.

Remember, out of the abundance of the heart the mouth speaks; so, you must be careful about what takes root in your heart. If you have developed a root of bitterness in your heart toward someone or a certain people, it can be removed with a heart transplant. Second Corinthians 5:17 (NJKV) says," therefore, if anyone is in Christ, he is a new creation; old things have passed away; behold, all things have become new. Is there someone that you can share that scripture with, or is it you that need to hear it? It doesn't matter what you were in the past.

You could have been a failure, a loser, a drunkard, sexual immoral, or addicted to any number of things. However, once you receive Jesus Christ into your life, you get a chance to start all over again. You are a brand-new person and a brand-new creation in Jesus Christ. You now find your identity in Christ and in his word. You are a brand-new person, fully equipped to live a victorious life. You may ask yourself, is it really that easy? Yes, it is.

The wonderful thing about this heart transplant that I'm referring to is that there is no waiting lists, there is no astronomical fee, you don't have to go through a painful surgery, no recovery room to wait in, you don't even have to leave your home. My friend, you can receive a heart transplant right now, right here this very minute, and it's free because the price has been prepaid already for you; and all you must do is ask for it.

Believe it and receive it, because all things are possible to them that believe. Be encouraged today my friends because God loves you.

Remember what he said," I will give you a new heart and put a new spirit within you; I will take the heart of stone out of your flesh and give you a heart of flesh. Here is the million-dollar question, are you ready for a character transformation?

Encouraged to take off the old broken man and put on the new man.

THERE ARE SO MANY PROFOUND lessons to be learned from life experiences, if we would only open our heart and mind to God as he speaks to us through these experiences. Life lessons that are invaluable teachers, which leads us to a clearer understanding of God's purpose for our lives. I woke up early this morning to pray and seek God for my day, my mind was full of trouble, doubt, and fear. I felt as though I was stuck in this mindset, and as I begin to pray all I could say was," Jesus, Jesus, Jesus." As I called upon the name of Jesus, he showed up. When he showed up, he brought to my remembrance an incident that occurred this past weekend.

My friend and I took my boat out to Silver Lake this past weekend, it was a wonderful day on the lake and there were many other boaters enjoying the last warm day. I was ready to put the pedal to the metal, but she was afraid to go very fast, so I had to drive rather slowly because there were a lot of waves. We engaged in conversation and I just allowed the boat to drift, we drifted up on a sandbar without my knowing it. After a while, I wondered why we weren't moving. Then I realized we were in 3 feet of water with the propeller stuck in the mud, and all types of thoughts ran through my mind.

I knew I had to get us back to the deeper water, so my only option was to hit the throttle and hope for the best. We kicked up so much sand and muck, and we did make it back to deeper water, but there was a problem. When I made it to deeper water I was at full throttle, but the boat was not picking up speed and it did not plane. My instincts told me to stop the boat, raise the motor and inspect the propeller. When I raised the motor, I saw the damage that I had done to the propeller as I tried to get us off the sandbar. All three blades on the propeller were broken, bent out of shape, and destroyed.

So that answered my question, as to why the boat was not picking up speed. So, we had to go very slow back to the boat ramp to put the boat back on the trailer to take it home. That was my life experience that happened over the weekend, and as I prayed this morning that experience was brought back to my mind. Then Jesus spoke to my heart and said," go take off the old broken propeller and put on a new stronger and better one." Of course, that would be the only logical thing to do. But there was a spiritual principle in this life lesson that I needed to understand about the broken blades on the propeller.

So, I immediately stopped praying, went outside to the garage and took off the old broken, and chewed up propeller and replaced it with a newer stronger one that I had years earlier. The spiritual lesson that I learned from this life experience, was that our lives can be like the boat that unintentionally drifts up on the sandbars of life and gets stuck. Then we destroy our mind, body and spirit in an attempt get free from the sandbars of life, only to realize that our lives have been so damaged that it is almost unrepairable. I said that our lives are almost unrepairable, Paul said in Second Corinthians 5:17(NJKV)," therefore if any man be in Christ, he is a new creature: old things are passed away; behold, all things are become new."

When I think about how damaged that old propeller was that I took off the boat, I realize that without a new one my boat was totally useless. It's the same principle with my life, I had to take off the old broken, bent out of shape, stuck in the mud mindset that I once had and exchange it for the mind of Christ. One of the greatest kings in the Bible had gotten stuck in the sandbar of life and was broken. King David himself had to adhere to this same principle with his broken mindset. In Psalms 51:10 (NJKV) he said," create in me a clean heart O God; and renew a right spirit within me." He had to take off the old and exchange it for the new.

In the book of Ezekiel 36:26-27 (NKJV) says," a new heart also will I give you, and a new spirit will I put within you: and I will take away the stony heart out of your flesh, and I will give you a heart of flesh. And I will put my spirit within you and cause you to walk in my statues and you shall keep my judgments and do them." My friends, sometimes the currents in the river of life will cause you to drift off course. Be encouraged, let not your heart be troubled, because you can put on the new man through faith in Christ alone. Be encouraged.

Encouraged to be Good Samaritans

LAST WEEK IN PARIS THE example of Good Samaritans was seen on national TV and across the World Wide Web. It was such a blessing to see men that were not afraid to lay down their lives for perfect strangers and disregard their own life and safety for the sake of others. The incident occurred on a train bound for Paris. Spencer Stone, Alek Skarlatos, Anthony Sadler, heard a shot on the train and went to investigate. They saw a man with an AK-47 that was jammed, and the man struggled desperately to get the weapon to fire.

Then Alek hit Spencer on the shoulder and said Let's go, three Good Samaritans that were ready to go the extra mile for their neighbors, even at risk of their own lives to save others. They were awarded medals of Honor for their heroic deeds, but I believe they have a greater reward coming. I'm reminded of the parable of the Good Samaritan in the Book of Luke, chapter 10:25 -37 (NKJV). Here Jesus gives the two greatest commandments," you shall love the Lord your God with all your heart, with all your soul, with all your strength, with all your mind, and your neighbor as yourself."

But the man wanting to justify himself, said to Jesus, who is my neighbor? Then Jesus answered and said:" A certain man went down from Jerusalem to Jericho, and fell among thieves, who stripped him of his clothing, wounded him, and departed, leaving him half dead. Now by chance a certain priest came down that road and when he saw him, he passed on the other side. Likewise, a Levite and when he arrived at the place, came and looked, and passed by on the other side.

But a certain Samaritan, as he journeyed, came where he was and when he saw him he had compassion on him. So, he went to him and bandaged his wounds, pouring on oil and wine; and he set him on his own animal, brought him to an inn, and took care of him. On the next day, when he departed, he took out two denarii, gave them to the innkeeper, and said to him, take care of him; and whatever more you spend, when I come again, I will repay you.

Which of these three do you think was neighbor to him who fell among the thieves? The man he said," he who showed mercy on him." Then Jesus said to him," go and do likewise." The three Good Samaritans on the train fulfill the second greatest commandment. Which is to love your neighbor as yourself. They were willing to lay down their lives for their neighbors, and to disregard their own personal safety. This was truly an act of selflessness, and love for their neighbor as they love themselves.

It is so important to God to break down the barriers of prejudice and hatred which often stands in the way of fulfilling God's two Great Commandments, that we love him and that we love one another. Prejudice is frequently one of hatred's powerful assistants. The Bible makes it clear that in Christ God sees all people alike and to think otherwise is to be deceived.

When Jesus ministered to the woman of Samaria, he was showing us that the barriers that exist between people, barriers of race, color, social views, economic, gender, and a host of other things people used to separate themselves can be crossed by God's love. Humans were not originally created to have walls between its members that would prevent people from love, and each another. These were introduced by the fall and now can be removed only in Christ. Be encouraged, we have the power to love one another through Christ Jesus.

Encouraged to be the hands of Christ

I READ A STORY BY Billy Graham in his Breakfast with Billy Graham Daily Reading, and he told a very interesting story. He said," in the city of Strasburg, Germany, is a church that was bombed during World War II. It was destroyed, but a statue of Christ which stood by the altar was almost unharmed. Only the hands of the statue are missing. The people of the church rebuilt their sanctuary, and a famous sculptor offered to make new hands to attach to the arms of the statue. But after considering the matter, the people decided to let the statue be, without hands.

They said, "Christ has no hands but ours to do his work on earth. If we don't feed the hungry, give drink to the thirsty, entertain the stranger, visit the imprisoned, and clothe the naked, who will?" Doctrine is important. But the Bible also teaches the importance of doing the work of Jesus Christ. This is the key phase," Christ has no hands but ours to do his work on earth." We must also consider our true purpose in life. Jesus came to serve, and that means if we are his people we are to serve also. I oversee a program called Breakfast & Hoops, this program is operated in a school where 96% of the students receive free or reduced lunch.

In this poverty-stricken neighborhood, at risk youth and families come twice a month to recreate and to enjoy a home cooked meal that is prepared, delivered, and served by the volunteers of a local church. This group has been sponsoring this event for the past 10 years, and they prepare breakfast for 75 – 125 people every other Saturday morning. This team of faithful volunteer's coordinator is the Deacon of a local church, who is a humble servant that is allowing himself and his team to be the hands of Christ in this neighborhood. In the entire 10 years they have only failed to show up 2 or 3 times, and that was because they were giving away turkeys and Thanksgiving baskets at their own church.

This Deacon and his team not only serve at our Breakfast & Hoops program, but they also do volunteer work at other venues around the city. This faithful group of volunteers are the perfect example of being the hands of Christ. Another program that I oversee is called," The Feeding Families Program. In this program we give food to needy families, seniors, single parents, caregivers, and grandparents. We have other volunteers that come to assist us in this endeavor to feed people that come to receive food. Sometimes the attitudes and ungratefulness of some of the participants are just overwhelming, but that's the nature of some of the people that you will deal with when you are a servant.

It's impossible to please all the people all the time, no matter what you do someone is not going to be happy with your decision. You would think that all the people would be so happy with the amount of the food they received, and there are still some that remain ungrateful but that doesn't stop us from serving. Last year we gave away 665,000 pounds of food in that neighborhood, but there were still recipients that were unsatisfied.

Mother Teresa said it well," People are unreasonable, illogical and self-centered. Love them anyway. If you do good, people will accuse you of selfish ulterior motives. Do good anyway. If you are successful, you win false friends and true enemies. Succeed anyway. The good you do today will be forgotten tomorrow. Do good anyway. Honesty and frankness make you vulnerable. Be honest and frank anyway. What you spend years building may be destroyed overnight. Build anyway. People really need help, but they may attack you if you help them. Help them anyway. Give the world the best you have, and you'll get kicked in the teeth. Give the world the best you've got anyway".

We've been called to be the hands of Christ and that means to serve, but sometimes serving is not easy. It's just as Mother Teresa said," People really need help but may attack you if you help them. Help them anyway. Being the hands of Christ means looking beyond the color barriers, the social and economic barriers, spiritual and physical barriers, also gender and cultural barriers. Jesus need our hands that will reach out to the poor in their lowest state of being, to serve with love and compassion. Jesus need our hands to hold the hands of the lonely, the broken, the elderly, the outcast, the hopeless, and the homeless.

Jesus need hands that will grasp the hands of the fatherless children that society has forgotten, and guild them down the path of life. Jesus need hands to wipe the tears stained eyes of those that are hurting and in pain, he need hands to reach out with compassion to a broken generation that has lost its moral compass. Jesus need hands that will tear down the mountain of hatred and prejudice that has grown and separated families, friends, and neighbors. Jesus need hands that will build bridges, not walls.

These hands will come in all colors, shapes, and sizes, some will be smooth and tender, some will be coarse and rough, some will be old and wrinkle, some will be dry and cracked, some will be scarred.

But they all will be gentle and kind. The only question is, will you extend your hands and allow yourself to be the hands of Jesus Christ to your neighbor? Be encouraged my friends, Christ has called you for such a time as this and he has empowered you to serve. Serve on my brothers and sisters.

Encouraged to add the main ingredient to your life

WHEN I WAS A CHILD in Mississippi, I loved to watch my mother make my favorite cakes. She would fill the bowl with the flour, add milk, then she would crack the eggs, and add the butter and the vanilla flavoring. Then she would say to me, "now what's missing?' and I knew she meant for me to give her the sugar. I knew that the main ingredient of the cake was the sugar, because without the sugar that cake wouldn't taste very good. The sugar is what made the cake the cake, and without it you had nothing that even came close to tasting like a cake. It's like apple juice without the apple, or like going swimming when there's no water in the pool.

Our lives are like the cake recipe, it contains ingredients that add character, personality, and goodness that flavors our lives. But unfortunately, sometimes we fail to add the main ingredient that makes our lives complete; and that ingredient is a sweet relationship with our Lord and Savior Jesus Christ. You will never know how sweet the relationship is until you have experienced it for yourself. In Psalm 34:8 (NKJV) King David said," Oh taste and see that the Lord is good." Have you ever been to a supermarket when a company was handing out free samples of their product? The basic concept behind this form of marketing is "try it; you'll like it."

The assumption is that once you've tried the product, you'll come back for more. King David assumed the same thing about one's experience with the Lord when he said," Oh taste and see that the Lord is good." David challenged people to, "taste and see that the Lord is good." He wanted them to taste God's goodness, because he wanted them to experience God firsthand. Baking a cake for your family is a labor of love but also basic chemistry, you are mixing ingredients together to make it into something wonderful. While leaving out the butter, the eggs, or the baking powder can change how the cake looks and taste, also If the main ingredient is left out which is the sugar, then what you have left is a horrible tasting flat piece of nothing.

After my mother was done adding all the ingredients, she would put this big bowl on her side, and begin to walk around the kitchen stirring it to mix it thoroughly together. Then, when she was done after about ten minutes of stirring, she would give me the spoon from the batter, that was dripping with this goodness that she had just prepared as a reward for my participation in the process. It tasted so good, that I think I would have eaten the spoon if she had not taken it from me when she saw I was done licking it clean. She knew how to add the right ingredients to make the cake do what it was supposed to do.

I've gotten busted many times trying to sneak a piece of that cake without permission, thank God for Grace and Mercy because they saved my life many days from my mother's wrath. I remember when my life didn't taste so good, because of all the wrong ingredients that I was adding to it. My life was just like that cake recipe before the sugar was added, it looked and tasted horrible because I forgot to add the main ingredient to it. All the wrong choices that I was making, and all the wrong ingredients that I was choosing from the shelves of the world trying to add flavor to my life and make it taste better.

I tried just about every kind of, (quote on quote) spice of life, but my life was still missing something. Have you ever tasted a dish and realized that an ingredient was missing? But you just couldn't put your finger on it, you knew there was a missing ingredient, but you kept drawing a blank as to what it was. That's where I was in my life, until I realized I was missing the main ingredient that would add a taste to my life that is like no other taste in the world.

There's a song that says," there is something about that name of Jesus, it's the sweetest name I know." I understand now because of the cakes that my mother used to make for me, that there is an ingredient that you must have in your life that will make all the difference in the world. Oh, taste and see that the Lord is good, and never again will you want to live without Him in your life. Be encouraged my friends, the spice of life awaits you. Add the main ingredient to your life, which is Jesus Christ.

Encouraged to get in where you fit in

WE ALL HAVE GIFTS THAT God has endowed us with, and these gifts make us uniquely different and very important to the Kingdom of God. Proverb 18:16 (NKJV) says,' A man's gift makes room for him, and brings him before great men.' There are gifts that have never been open, and the owner of the gift is oblivious of the joy and beauty that is emanated from this very special package. Your gift will make room for you, because there is a place that is designed specifically for your unique gift and calling. When God created us, He had a purpose in mind for us, but we get so distracted from the task that we lose our focus.

It's like when Peter walked on the water to go to Jesus, when he kept his eyes on Jesus he walked on the water, but as soon as he took his eyes off Jesus he began to sink. It is the same way with us, if we get distracted we are unable to utilize our gifts to its fullest and thus, the distraction causes us to take our eyes off what we should be focusing on. It is at that precise moment that we begin to sink beneath the waves of life troubles. All the situations and circumstances that are occurring in the world today, can and will cause us to lose our focus. Therefore, we lose our peace of mind.

Isaiah 26:3 (NKJV) says," You will keep him in perfect peace, whose mind is stayed on you, because he trusts in you." We cannot get in where we fit in, if we are not in perfect peace. Perfect peace brings you to a place where you can clearly understand your situation and make the necessary adjustments that will bring your life into alignment with your purpose. God created us with a specific purpose in mind, and his desire is for us to fulfill our purpose that we might bring glory to him.

We cannot bring glory to God when we are angry, fearful, or doubtful. God wants us to move pass our selfish nature and desires, because he knows that we cannot reach the epitome of success if we stay in our old selfish nature. The place that God has ascribed for us will make room for us and bring recognition to him and success to our lives. Moses, Abraham, Joshua, David, Daniel, Gideon, and Elijah, just to name a few of the men of the Old Testament that were brought before kings. Their gifts made room for them to sit before great men and bring glory to God. New Testament Apostles also used their gifts to sit among great men and exact change for God.

There is a place that God has called you too, where you can make changes in a situation that will bring glory and honor to God also, while enhancing the lives of all those around you. God wants you to know that your gift will sit you at the table of great men, but it is to promote God's agenda, God's will, and God's purpose. Be encouraged my friends, you will get in where you fit in, if you allow God to come in.

Let your faith be bigger than your fear

I HEARD A STORY ONCE about a little girl that was asked this question, "what would you do if Satan came and knocked on your door?" She said," I would let Jesus answer the door." You would probably say," what else would you expect a little girl to say, because she would definitely be afraid of Satan." No doubt she would be afraid, but her faith was bigger than her fears. Let me explain, I encounter situations in my everyday life that causes me to be just like that little girl, with problems and uncertainties that intimidate and threaten me. I'm a big guy, and at 6'3 and 200 and (I'm not telling) pounds, even for me life can be scary.

Yet, I have learned just like that little girl, that when I am afraid I must allow my faith to be bigger than my fears. In 2nd Corinthians 5:7 (NKJV) says" for we walk by faith, and not by sight." When we walk by sight, problems seem bigger than what they really are. But when we walk by faith, it doesn't matter how big the problem is. Because you remember what 1st John 4:4 (NKJV) says, "You are of God, little children, and have overcome them, because He that is in you, is greater than he that is in the world." That verse my brothers and sisters is the key that should unlock our faith and allows it to be grow bigger than our fears.

When our faith grows bigger than our fears, it is not you or I that answers the door when trouble knocks, but it is the Jesus in us that answers the door. You must remember my friends, that this great power that is in you is greater than any power on earth, no demons in hell or on the earth can defeat that power that lives within you. Your faith is greater than any fear that you will ever encounter, so be not afraid but encourage yourself in the Lord.

The story of Daniel in the lion's den is the perfect example of faith, when it is larger than fear. Daniel's faith was larger than his life, and others around him saw this and they despised him for it. But God rewarded him for his faithfulness and showed his favor on Daniel's life openly that others might see the goodness of God. Let me paraphrase the story found in Daniel 6:1-28 (NKJV). Daniel's coworkers hated him because he had an excellent spirit in him, this excellent spirit was the spirit of God that dwelled within Daniel. Remember the story of the little girl that was asked," what would she do if Satan knocked on the door? Her reply was," I will let Jesus answer the door."

That little girl had what Daniel had, she had an excellent spirit dwelling within her that caused her faith to be larger than her fear. Daniel's coworkers devised a scheme to kill two birds with one stone. In other words, they wanted to kill Daniel and place the King in a position that he could not change the law that they wanted him to decree. Unfortunately, those envious coworkers knew of Daniel's faith, but they didn't know the power of Daniel's God. Even after the King had signed the decree that could not be changed, he said to Daniel," Your God that you serve continually, he will deliver you."

So, they placed Daniel in the lion's den, and covered it with a large stone. Early the next morning the King rushed to the lion's den, and he asked the question," O Daniel, servant of the living God, is your God, who you serve continually able to deliver you from the lions?" Then Daniel said to the King," My God has sent his angel, and has shut the mouth of the lions, that they have not hurt me." The presence of the angel of the Lord, caused Daniel's faith to be bigger than his fear. Those very coworkers that meant evil for good was rewarded with the evil, but Daniel was rewarded with the good and God was glorified. Be encouraged my friends, when trouble knocks on the door, let the Jesus in you answer the door and he will make your faith greater than your fear.

Don't Judge the Book by the Cover

HAVE YOU EVER JUDGED A book without reading it first, or just by looking at the cover? Have you ever judged a problem without hearing the entire matter? Have you ever judged a movie by the first few scenes of the movie? Have you ever looked at a person, and without them ever saying a word judged their character? Maybe you are one of the fortunate people that don't judged the book by the cover, because you process the perception to see beyond the semblance. I myself, still struggle with the idea of" what you see, is what you get." Which I've learned is not always the case. Wisdom, my friend does not necessarily come with age, most of the time it will come through life experiences.

The Bible tells us not to judge another person, but we do it regularly without even realizing that we are engaged in sin. In the seventh chapter of the book of Matthew, the very first verse says," Judge not, that you be not judged." I don't know about you, but I am guilt of judging other people, based on how they look, how they speak, and the stereotypical image that the world holds about that person or their culture. Although I am judged similarly, I have no right to reciprocate in like fashion as others. A book could be wrapped in a gold covering with letters of silver, and yet its contents are filled with words and thoughts that destroys the human spirit.

On the other hand, a book can look plain and simple and yet, reveal words of profound wisdom and beauty that will elevate its readers mind to new dimensions. The same analogy can be applied to humanity also. You can't judge a book by the cover. There is an individual where I work that I judged prematurely, because he is of a different nationality and culture. I would see him almost daily, but I would walk pass him without saying a word. I thought that I could exist without talking to this person, but I was so wrong. You must understand, I am the encourager and that's what I do. Although, sometimes the encourager needs encouraging, and who do you think that God chose to encourage me?

Would you believe the same man that I walked past almost every day without saying a word, he would be the one to encourage me in my time of need? It wasn't really a time of need, but rather a time of panic on my part. We were both sitting in the hot tub at a facility, I didn't have anything to say to this individual, and then I dropped my locker keys in the hot tub and for some reason I panicked. Then it happened, this man that I had never spoken to said to me, "Don't worry, it will be ok." Those six word that he said brought a calm to my spirit that I will never forget.

After I retrieved my keys from the bottom of the hot tub, I asked him his name, and he told me that his name was Eddie. I asked him where he was from, and he said, "he was from Israel. "Then I began to tell him my name and that I was an encourager of other people, but today, he had just encouraged me with those six words. I told him how important his words of encouragement were to me at that time, and that we all need encouragement sometimes in our lives. Eddie turned out to be a very friendly guy, and I would have never known this had I not dropped my keys in the hot tub that day.

We should never judge a book by the cover, it may look totally different on the inside. Dr. Martin Luther King once said, "Don't judge me by the color of my skin, but by the content of my character." How many of God's people have we misjudged because of the color of their skin? Or because they don't look like we look, or talk like we talk, or they don't go to the same church that we go to or worship the same way that we do. God did not call believers in Christ to judge other people! There is only one judge, and that is God. Christians have been called to love other people.

Tragically, there are some Christians whose lives are characterized by smallness of heart, judgmentalism, condemnation, and criticism of others. Our hearts are to be so filled with God's love for others that we literally "fall in love" with them. The mark of every Christian is to have a strong and noble love for others. Remember friends, take the log out of your eye and then you can see clearly to take the speck from the other person's eye. Be encouraged, and don't judge the book by the cover.

Faith to believe

I REMEMBER MY CHILDHOOD GROWING up in Chicago, and after joining a street gang and bringing a gun into the house. I can still hear my mother saying," boy I'm going to give you to the Lord." I never knew exactly what that meant until later in my life, when I had time to look back over my life too see where God had brought me from and what he brought me through. My mother was short in stature, but she was a giant in faith, she was a churchgoing praying woman. I never knew where my mom got her faith from, but it was anchored in the hope of our Lord and Savior Jesus Christ.

I never really made time to get to know my mom or her favorite things, like what was her favorite food? Or what was her favorite color? Because I was too busy learning the ways of the world instead of learning the ways of my favorite girl, my mom. My mother loved me with a passion and that I know, she would've given her life for me; but I was too busy to realize just how special God had made her and how strong and determined she was. I didn't know it at the time, but my mom had given me one of the greatest gifts a parent can give their child.

She dedicated me to the Lord when she said," boy I'm going to give you too the Lord." I did not know that It was more than a statement that my mother had made, it was an official surrendering me to God. I was the only child that my mother ever had, she was 14 years old when I was born and I'm sure that I was a handful because she was still just a baby. I never did learn the full story behind my mother's pregnancy because it was a well-kept secret, but God knew all about it and he had his own plans and purpose for my life that was conceived in secret.

There is a story in the Bible in the book of 1st Samuel chapter 1, that tells about a mother named Hannah who also dedicated her son to the Lord. In the 11th verse of 1st Samuel it says," then she made a vow and said, "O Lord of hosts, if you will indeed look on the affliction of your maidservant and remember me, and not forget your maidservant, but will give your maidservant a male child, then I will give him to the Lord all the days of his life. In the 2nd chapter of 1st Samuel you can read Hannah's prayer to God in response to her answered prayer.

Hannah's prayer reveals that God can take negative and hopeless situations and turn them around completely. Hannah rejoices because she realizes that her life was in the hand of Almighty God who delights in answering the prayers of his people no matter how small and insignificant those problems may seem.

I thank God for my mother, because she had the faith to believe beyond who I was in my stupidity and to commit my life to the Lord. She knew that God had the power to turn my life around and she believed it was more in me than I could see or realized at that time in my life; she knew that God had a plan and a purpose for my life. My mother had faith to believe that God would use me for a much greater purpose than destroying the lives of others, her hope was anchored in God to deliver her only son from the hands of the enemy who came to steal, to kill, and to destroy.

My mother believed that Jesus came that we might have life, and that more abundantly. She had faith to believe that my life had a greater purpose than in the cotton fields of Mississippi, she believed that my life had a greater purpose than to be consumed by the street gangs of Chicago, the drugs, jails and prisons, she believed that there was more in me than I could see. My mother was right, there was more and still is so much more within me that God wants to use. He gave me talents, skills, and abilities at birth to point the way to his son Jesus Christ who can reveal the true purpose for your life.

My dear mother passed away before she saw me become an ordained minister and pastor, and the thousands of lives that God has touch through the ministry that He gave me; but God allowed her to see what was in me before it came to be. I thank God for my mother who dedicated me to the Lord that I might be use for his glory, be encouraged my friends, and have faith to believe.

Faith that Leads

HEBREWS CHAPTER 11:6 (NKJV) SAYS, "Faith is the substance of things hoped for, the evidence of things not seen." Another biblical figure in the Bible that found himself in a faith stretching place was King Jehoshaphat, his account is found in 2nd Chronicles 20:1 (NKJV). It happened after this that the people of Moab with the people of Ammon, and others with them besides the Ammonites, came to battle against Jehoshaphat. And Jehoshaphat feared, and set himself to seek the Lord, and proclaimed a fast throughout all Judah."

The Bible clearly states that Jehoshaphat was afraid, but he set himself to seek the Lord. When fear comes into our mind it brings the flight or fight syndrome into play, because fear has two meanings. (#1). Fear can cause you to forget everything and run. Or, (#2). Face everything and rise. Matthew 6:33 (NKJV) says," Seek first the kingdom of God, and his righteousness, and all these things shall be added unto you."

King Jehoshaphat could have rallied his troops together, but he knew that he was greatly outnumbered three to one, he knew that this battle was impossible for him to win, but he knew that God could bring him through this faith stretching place. Faith serves as an anchor and when we are firmly anchored in God, the anchor holds despite the storms that we are going through.

King Jehoshaphat's confidence was not in his army, or the weapons at his disposal, his confidence was in the Lord God Almighty. 2nd Chronicles 17:3 (NKJV) says," Now the Lord was with Jehoshaphat, because he walked in the former ways of his father David; he did not seek the Baals, but sought the God of his father, and walked in His commandments and not do according to the acts of Israel. King Jehoshaphat remembered that the Lord God was with him before, and he remembered if God was for him, he would have the victory.

It's easy to be blinded by overwhelming odds, and situations that loom over us like towering mountains, the Bible is full of men and women that stood their ground and received the victories in the face of insurmountable odds, and we can do the same when we face our battles. We are told," to walk by faith and not by sight," but so many of us tell God how big our problems are; as if they were too big for God to solve them.

Instead, we should be telling our problems how big our God is, and that nothing is too hard for our God. When was the last time that you stood up to your giant and stared it in the eyes and said," peace, be still, and no weapon formed against me shall prosper." In 2nd Chronicles 20:6 (NKJV) King Jehoshaphat said," O Lord God of our fathers, are you not God in heaven, and do you not rule over all the kingdoms of the nations, and in your hand, is there not power and might, so that no one is able to withstand you?

Verse 9 says," If disaster comes upon us sword, judgment, pestilence, or famine we will stand before this temple and in your presence (for your name is in this temple), and cry out to you in our affliction, and you will hear and save. Verse 12 says," O our God, will you not judge them? For we have no power against this great multitude that is coming against us; nor do we know what to do, but our eyes are upon you." Have you ever been so afraid and concerned about a situation that you went to your mother, your father, your family, and everyone except God?

Remember what Matthew 6:33 (NKJV) says," Seek first the kingdom of God and his righteousness, and all these things shall be added unto you." Let your eyes be upon God because he has the power to change the outcome of any situation that you may face. Verse 14a says," then the spirit of the Lord came upon Jahaziel the son of Zachariah. Verse 15 says," And he said," Listen, all of you of Judah and you inhabitants of Jerusalem, and you, King Jehoshaphat! Thus, says the Lord to you: Do not be afraid nor dismayed because of this great multitude, for the battle is not yours, but God's."

Verse 17 says," you will not need to fight in this battle. Position yourselves, stand still and see the salvation of the Lord, who is with you, O Judah and Jerusalem! Do not fear or be dismayed; tomorrow go out against them, for the Lord is with you. Verse 20 says," so they rose early in the morning and went out into the wilderness of Tekoa; and as they went out, Jehoshaphat stood and said, "Hear me, O Judah and you inhabitants of Jerusalem: Believe in the Lord your God, and you shall be established; believe his prophets, and you shall prosper."

Believe, (ah-mahn): To be firm, stable, established; also, to be firmly persuaded; to believe solidly. Jehoshaphat boldly declared to the people God's unchangeable covenant amid a crisis: "Believe in the Lord your God, and you shall be established; believe his prophets, and you shall prosper."

Through Jehoshaphat, God told the people that they could depend on him and on his word. Verse 22 says," now when they began to sing and to praise, the Lord set ambushes against the people of Ammon, Moab, and Mount Seir, who had come against Judah; and they were defeated." Not only does praise usher in the presence of the Lord, it defeats the enemy. One of the most remarkable battles in history,

Jehoshaphat, king of Judah, appointed singers and sent them out before the Army.

When they begin to sing and to praise, the Lord set ambushes against the people of Ammon. Moab, and Mount Sier. Satan and his demons hate praise. Perhaps praise was the primary thing that Satan wanted when he rebelled against God. When he hears it coming from the lips of those who love the Lord, it, no doubt bothers him terribly. Demons flee when we praise the Lord. My friends, life will lead you into a faith stretching place; but you must remember that nothing is too hard for God.

Remember, if God brought you to it, He'll bring you through it and if you will trust him he will give you the victory. Until next time be encouraged my friends, ask God to increase your faith and he will.

Faith that Moves Mountains

HAVE YOU EVER HAD A mountain in your life that you just couldn't get over it, go around it, or through it? You did everything that you knew to do, and it still refused to move, no matter how hard you tried it just wouldn't move and no matter how hard you cried it remained immovable. I had a mountain like that in my life once and I was given all types of self-help tips, tips from hypnosis to therapy, from a patch that could be worn on my arm to all types of weird remedies to stop smoking. It was 26 years ago when I stopped smoking after I used many different methods to quit. One of my least favorite methods of quitting was what I called," the mooching method," this method called for me to mooch off other smokers instead of buying my own cigarettes every time I got the craving.

This method was very embarrassing, but it didn't stop me from smoking, it's only accomplishment was me receiving the evil eye from those that saw me coming to ask for a cigarette. Another method that I used was to buy a whole pack of cigarettes and only take five or six cigarettes out of the package and leave the rest at home. This method was called," the I think I can method," that method was short lived, because I would smoke all the cigarettes that I brought with me and I would revert to, "the Mooching Method."

Another method I developed was to smoke only half of the

cigarette and save the other half for later, that was a bad idea because the other half of the cigarette that I saved and put in my pocket smelled so bad that I didn't even want to smoke it again later. That method was called," the Stinking Thinking Method." The next method that I tried was called," the Cold Turkey Method," using this method I would refuse to buy any cigarettes at all, and I would refuse to ask anyone for a cigarette. With this method, I would get so angry from withdrawals that the only one who would talk to me was my negative self-talking conscience. I soon lost interest in that method because my negative self-talking conscience would say things like," you are going to get fat," or," you are going to be as big as a house, and smoking will help you lose weight.

Finally, at my wits end I sought help outside of myself and other people. I turned to the Word of God and I read the words of Psalms 34:4-6 (NKJV) that said," I sought the Lord, and he heard me, and delivered me from all my fears. They looked to Him and were radiant, and their faces were not ashamed. This poor man cried out, and the Lord heard him, and saved him out of all his troubles. As I think back about my situation, I now know that I was afraid, in trouble and I thought that I could not live without smoking cigarettes. I was afraid that if I stop smoking I would get fat and I wouldn't fit in with the crowd anymore and I was afraid that I would be different.

You see, I had been playing Indian giver with God, I was saying to God," here God take this habit, no give it back," here God take this habit, no give it back." But when I started to walk by faith and not by sight, God came in and moved those mighty mountains out of my life that I did not have the power to move by myself. It happened on a Monday morning when I was off work and sitting in my living room praying, I asked God to take this habit from me because I didn't want to smoke anymore. I remember praying so hard that the shirt I had on was wet with sweat, and as I surrendered myself to Jesus Christ I heard in my spirit, when you take off that wet shirt you will take off that habit of smoking cigarettes that you have had on all those years.

On that day when I removed that wet shirt from my body in faith through God's word, God removed that old habit that I had struggled with for years and ever since that day I have never smoked another cigarette and that was over 26 years ago, faith can move a mighty mountain. My friends, what mountains are you facing in your life that seems immovable, with God nothing shall be impossible. Be encouraged my friends and have faith.

Faith that Displaces Fear

WHEN I WAS A CHILD in Mississippi we lived on a plantation, a plantation is an estate on which crops such as cotton is grown and cultivated by the residents that live on the owner's property. In the evening after the sun set it was very dark, and many evenings after supper I had to go get water from a well that was about half a block from our little house. At night, the only lights that were visible was that of the moon and a huge light overlooking the equipment shed that was about 20 yards from the location of the well. However, it was not enough light for a frightened 10-year-old boy with an over active imagination.

The older people would tell the children scary stories about a wild Boogeyman that roamed the woods of Mississippi, but I wasn't afraid when I had my best friend with me whose name was Big Track. He was a big brown and black Collie and Germen Shepherd mixed with the biggest paws you had ever saw. Big Track was the greatest friend there ever was, and he would follow me anywhere, especially if I gave him a bite of my mother's homemade biscuits.

I was a scary kid with a very active imagination, I was fearless during the daytime, but the darkness was my worst enemy because it would send three-headed monsters and one eyed purple people eaters to devour the flesh from my bones; fortunately, big track was always there to save me from the monsters that dwelled in the dark places in my head.

During those times in Mississippi we didn't have running water in the house, so I had to make frequent trips to the well to get water and big track would always go with me and protect me. After supper I always saved one of my mother's biscuits for the trip to the well. Years passed as I grew up and big track grew older, he eventually died and went across the rainbow bridge to doggie heaven. My friend big track took the fear out of the darkness when I was with him, my faith in him drove the fear away because I knew that he would protect me from my imaginary monsters.

Shortly after big track died we left Mississippi and moved to Chicago, that's when the bogeyman and the other monsters became real in my life in the form of drugs, alcohol, gangs, guns and violence, promiscuity and a host of other teen-age monsters. I didn't have big track to walk with me through the dark places of my teen-age years to protect me, and once again fear set in but this time it was a paralyzing fear.

I would wake up in the middle of the night with the covers over my head and I would be paralyzed with fear, it felt like something was sitting on top of me and I couldn't move, talk or scream for help. Fear had moved back in and my faith had moved out because I didn't have anyone to walk with me through my dark places. When we lived in Mississippi my mother took me to church every Sunday and I learn about faith in God, but when we moved to Chicago I stopped going to church because I was making my own decisions and most of them were the wrong decisions.

At age 16 I came home one night with a gun in my pocket and my mother said to me with tears running down her face," boy, I'm going to give you to the Lord." I really didn't know what that meant then, but I found out later in my life. I dropped out of school to get a job and to get married at age 17, and no she was not pregnant, but I thought that I was a man. After three children and a failed 18-year marriage my faith was nowhere to be found, fear was ever present, and I still had no one to walk with me through my dark places.

After life had chewed me up and spit me out, I remarried and renewed my faith at a small church in Milwaukee, fear was still present but as my faith grew bigger my fears grew smaller. As I surrounded myself with faithful believers in God and nourished myself with the Word of God, my faith returned, and my heart was opened to the great mercy and love that God had for me that fear tried to keep me away from. I had finally found someone who would walk with me through my dark places and his name was Jesus Christ.

I became unafraid of the monsters that were in the dark places in my mind and in the darkness of this world, and never again will I have to walk alone because He promised me that He will never leave me nor forsake me. I have learned that He is God and He cannot lie, be encouraged my friends and remember that God has not given you a spirit of fear, but of power, and of love and a sound mind.

Faith to Surrender

HAVE YOU EVER GOTTEN INTO a fight that you wish you hadn't? Only to realize that you came out on the wrong end of the fight. It happened to me when I was a child going to school in Mississippi, I don't quite remember how the fight started but I do remember he was a short kid that was as tough as nails. I remember him having a lot of brothers and sisters, but I was the only child in my family. Maybe if I had brothers and sisters they could have helped me in the worst fight of my life

I don't remember his name, but I do remember him giving me such a terrible thrashing. As I think back over my life I understand that I didn't know how to surrender, nor did I know that surrendering meant that I could've saved myself from the beat down I ever received. Later, in my teenage years I learned that waving a white flag was a sign of surrender and that no further harm would come to you. Had I known this, I would have been waving white flags all over the school's playground that day.

As I grew up I had a few other encounters, but nothing like that fight in Mississippi. I got stronger, wiser, tougher, and I didn't have any more fights in Mississippi. Then we moved to Chicago and it was a totally different world, I was the quiet odd-looking kid with sandy brown hair, dark skin, and with the country accent that everyone laughed at. I finally made some friends and got through middle school, but high school presented a challenge in the form of gangs, drugs and of course, bullies!! One of the bullies that I encountered was a gang leader that everyone was afraid of, but I didn't really know this guy until one day in the cafeteria he introduced himself to me in the wrong way.

I was sitting at the table with three friends talking and eating lunch, during that time in the late 60s most of the guys had their hair in a process. A process was a hairstyle that you achieved by putting chemicals in your hair to straighten it, it was the in thing to do and all the guys were wearing a process. I was sitting at the lunch table with my back to the door as he and his gang came in the lunch room, and he did the unthinkable to me. He messed up my hair, and I jumped up from the table with my hair standing up like a rooster in a barnyard, and I went after him without knowing who he was.

I really didn't care that he had four other guys with him because I was mad, and a big fight broke out in the cafeteria with me fighting a gang of thugs. After about thirty seconds into the fight I found myself on my back on the floor, surrounded by guys trying to stomp on my head. I really could have used a white flag at that moment. Once again God saved me by sending the basketball coach to get those guys off me. The gang leader and his gang were all suspended.

The fight in Mississippi and the fight in Chicago paled in comparison to the next challenger I was about to face, this challenger had knocked out many of my friends and family members. This challenger was strong, tough and surefooted, if you were not sure of yourself he would throw you a 1-2 punch and put you to sleep. I saw him take out some of the toughest guys from the mean streets of Chicago and turn them into bums and drug addicts. He beat them down so bad that they lost all dignity and self-respect, they lost sight of their dreams and goals, they even lost their ambition to succeed.

I dropped out of high school to got married and soon after that I met the biggest and toughest opponent I ever encountered, he was called Life and he truly did turn me every which way but loose. I'm only standing here today because I surrendered to God and He sent his Son Jesus Christ to save me, I waved the white flag of surrender and I excepted him as my Lord and Savior and he came in and gave me victory over every battle that I was fighting. I had faith to surrender to Jesus Christ, and he gave me power to be an overcomer. You can become an overcomer also by surrendering through faith in Jesus Christ, be encouraged my friends, have faith to surrender.

Faith that Guides

SEVERAL YEARS AGO, DURING ONE of my Evangelistic trips to Northern Wisconsin I had an opportunity to do some fishing, and as most people know Northern Wisconsin is known for its great variety of fish; especially bluegill and crappie. The resort that I occupied during my stay was known for its great bluegill and crappie population. I had an agenda and I was eager to decrease the population of the lake by as many slabs as my free time would allow, or by the limit that would keep me within the legal bounds of my fishing license.

The Pastor and his wife graciously guided me to the local bait store where I met the premier fishing guide. I was really impressed by all the mounted trophies that he had collected over the years and I said to myself this guy knows where the fish are. After he and I had talked for about 10 minutes, I told him where I was staying and how long I would be staying, he knew the area and the name of the lake and even showed me on the map where to go, and what time to be there to catch the biggest slabs and what type of bait to use.

I left bait shop so excited that I could hardly wait for the next morning to get up and go fishing. Finally, morning came, and I had everything all packed and ready to go, but when I got to the boat launch I realize that the boats didn't have motors. No problem, I was so pumped up, and filled with enthusiasm that I didn't need a motor to get to the spot on the map. The sun was just coming up, it was a beautiful day, I was going slab hunting and I was ready to divide and conquer. After about 20 minutes of rowing I finally made it to the other side of the lake, and I saw the spot that was marked on the map.

It was an area that was draped with lily pads and weeds, the perfect hiding place for slab bluegill and crappie. I could hardly wait to throw my line in the water and bring in the big one, it was the right time of morning, the right location, I had the right type of bait, and I was ready do this!!

I baited my hook and eagerly casted my line in the direction of the lily pads and weeds that were about 10 feet in front of the boat, my bluegill rig was now set up and waiting for a strike from a slab bluegill. Now to set up my crappie rig to lure some of those monster crappies in for a strike, I had my eyes on my bluegill bobber while I was casting for crappie with wide eyed anticipation of a strike at any moment now. After about 10 minutes I determined that I needed to move a little further into the lily pads and weeds, anxiousness and anticipation had a firm hold on me and I was captured by the idea that a strike was imminent.

An hour or so later I began to question my understanding of the directions, because the guide said if I were to go to this certain spot on the lake and use this type of bait at this time of morning I would catch slab bluegill and crappie. His directions were very clear, and I listened very well because I thought he was the expert in this area to lead me to accomplishing my desires of decreasing the slab bluegill and crappie population in this lake. After five hours of casting, pulling up anchor and relocating to different spots and not catching a single fish, I was ready to take the long journey back to the other side.

After an hour of slow rowing I finally made it back to the other side, misinformed, misdirected and no fish to show for my efforts of hard labor and of listening to the directions of the Northern Wisconsin fishing guide. I didn't catch any fish that day, but God did give me a message for his people about who should be guiding them in life and any other situations. The fishing guide's name was not on the list, we are to walk by faith and not by sight; nothing against the fishing guide or any other person, but we are not to put our faith in mankind to guide and direct our lives.

In Isaiah 58:11(NKJV)," and the Lord shall guide you continually, and satisfy your soul in drought, and make fat your bone: and you shall be like a watered garden, and like a spring of water, whose water never fails." Our faith will guide us if we will be obedient, because we have been given precious promises by God the father that will lead us through life from our birth to our death and he will never leave us nor misguide us. He is the divine guide and he knows how and where to lead his people; however difficult the places may be because no place is beyond his reach even to the borders of the unseen he will guide you with his eyes. Psalms 32:8 (NKJV), " I will instruct you and teach you in the way which you shall go: I will guide you with my eye". Be encouraged my friends, your faith will guide you.

Faith in the lion's den.

HOW STRONG IS YOUR FAITH? can it sustain you at the office when everyone is talking about you? Can it sustain you in a road rage episode? Can it sustain you when your kids are driving you up the wall? Can it sustain you when your coworkers are trying to derail you in every effort you make to be a great employee? Can it sustain you when you are in the enemy's camp? Can it sustain you in a den of hungry lion's?

In the sixth Chapter of Daniel (NKJV) we read about such faith that brought Daniel safely out of the lion's den. As the story goes Daniel was found faithful by king Darius who sought to promote him over the whole kingdom, but the other administrators and satraps tried to find grounds for charges against Daniel and his conduct of government affairs, but they were unable to do so. Keep in mind that when you are doing God's work and you are faithful, the enemy will do anything to derail and distract you from the appointed tasks that God has assigned to you.

I have never walked in a lion's den, but 12 years ago, I was diagnosed with rectal cancer and was told by my doctor that I needed surgery to have it removed, I was already familiar with this deadly beast called cancer. Earlier in my life this deadly beast had already claimed the life of my mother through thyroid cancer on February

13th, 1983, she was only 44 years old, then nine years later after my mother's death I lost my son on May 10, 1992 when this ravenous beast claimed his life through prostate cancer, he was just 19-year-old.

I saw this ravenous beast destroy my mother, and I watched as it consumed the life of my 19-year-old son. Then I too was in the den of this ravenous beast and all I had to rely on was my faith, and with the same power that God shut the lion's mouth in Daniels situation, he also did in my situation. My God did deliver me from the mouth of this beast called cancer, and my faith sustained me because I walked by faith and not by sight.

There will come a time when you also will have to walk through the lion dens of life, because life will test your faith to see how strong it is. Daniel knew that the decree had been written, and yet he prayed to his God despite the dire consequences that he would face. Nevertheless, Daniel was not afraid because he had saw the power of his God and he was confident that if God was for him it did not matter who was against him.

Daniel remembered when God delivered Shadrach, Meshach, and Abed-Nego from the fiery furnace, when King Nebuchadnezzar said to them in Daniel 3:14 (NKJV)," is it true that you do not serve my God's or worship the gold image which I have set up? They said to the king in Daniel 3:16-17 (NKJV)," we have no need to answer you in this matter," if that is the case, the God whom we serve is able to deliver us from the burning fiery furnace and he will deliver us from your hands O king.

When the doctor told me that I had cancer I was afraid, but I remembered all that God had brought me through and I found confidence in God, to trust him with my life because after all my life was in his hands. Faith only looks back to remember how far it has come, and each time I looked back I remembered that God was at the wheel. Friends, not only will your faith take you through the lion's den, it will take you over mountains that look insurmountable, and across deserts that look like Death Valley, but you must remember that with God nothing is impossible.

Daniel refused to worship any but the true God; and he continued to pray to God, Daniel's obedience to God caused him something, and he was thrown into the lion's den to be devoured. Once again, God honored Daniel's faithfulness to him and sent an angel to shut the mouth of the lions. The new king was sympathetic to Daniel, but his evil advisors had tricked him into trying to kill him. Immediately, he ordered all those who wanted Daniel to be sent into the lion's den to be sent there themselves. Then he passed the law that everybody and his kingdom must worship Daniels God. Because of Daniel's faithfulness, God caused him to prosper in the land.

If you will be faithful and true to God, God will be faithful to you in your time of need. God said," he will never leave you nor forsake you." All he asks of you is to trust hm. Until next time my friends, be encouraged and keep the faith.

Faith to believe

I REMEMBER MY CHILDHOOD GROWING up in Chicago, and after joining a street gang and bringing a gun into the house I can still hear my mother saying," boy I'm going to give you to the Lord." I never knew exactly what that meant until later in my life, when I had time to look back over my life too see where God had brought me from and what He brought me through. My mother was short in stature, but she was a giant in faith, she was a churchgoing praying woman. I never knew where my mom got her faith from, but it was anchored in the hope of our Lord and Savior Jesus Christ.

I never really made time to get to know my mom or her favorite things, like what was her favorite food? Or what was her favorite color? Because I was too busy learning the ways of the world instead of learning the ways of my favorite girl, my mom. My mother loved me with a passion and that I know, she would've given her life for me; but I was too busy to realize just how special God had made her and how strong and determined she was. I didn't know it at the time, but my mom had given me one of the greatest gifts a parent can give their child.

She dedicated me to the Lord when she said," boy I'm going to give you too the lord." I did not know that It was more than a statement that my mother had made, it was an official surrendering of my life to God. I was the only child that my mother ever had, she was 14 years old when I was born and I'm sure that I was a handful because she was still just a baby. I never did learn the full story behind my mother's pregnancy because it was a well-kept secret, but God knew all about it and he had his own plans and purpose for my life that was conceived in secret.

There is a story in the Bible in the book of 1st Samuel Chapter 1, that tells about a mother named Hannah who also dedicated her son to the Lord. In 1st Samuel 1:11(NKJV) it says," then she made a vow and said, "O Lord of hosts, if you will indeed look on the affliction of your maidservant and remember me, and not forget your maidservant, but will give your maidservant a male child, then I will give him to the Lord all the days of his life. In the 2nd Chapter of 1st Samuel you can read Hannah's prayer to God in response to her answered prayer. Hannah's prayer reveals that God can take negative and hopeless situations and turn them around completely. Hannah rejoices because she realizes that her life was in the hand of Almighty God who delights in answering the prayers of his people no matter how small and insignificant those problems may seem.

I thank God for my mother, because she had the faith to believe beyond who I was in my stupidity and to commit my life to the Lord. She knew that God had the power to turn my life around and she believed it was more in me than I could see or realize at that time in my life; she knew that God had a plan and a purpose for my life. My mother had faith to believe that God would use me for a much greater purpose than destroying the lives of others, her hope was anchored in God to deliver her only son from the hands of the enemy who came to steal, to kill, and to destroy.

My mother believed that Jesus came that we might have life, and that more abundantly. She had faith to believe that my life had a greater purpose than in the cotton fields of Mississippi, she believed that my life had a greater purpose than to be consumed by the street gangs of Chicago, the drugs, jails and prisons, she believed that there was more in me than I could see. My mother was right, there was more and still is so much more within me that God wants to use. He gave me talents, skills, and abilities at birth to point the way to his son Jesus Christ who can reveal the true purpose for your life.

My dear mother passed away before she saw me become an Ordained Minister and Pastor, and the thousands of lives that God has touch through the ministry that God gave me; but God allowed her to see what was in me before it came to be. I thank God for my mother who dedicated me to the Lord that I might be use for his glory, be encouraged my friends, and have faith to believe that God has a divine purpose for your life also.

Faith that Reaches Beyond the Break

I HEARD A STORY ONCE about a father that couldn't swim, and one day his only son was swimming in the river near their home when he got into trouble and began to drown. As the father stood on the bank of the river, unable to swim out and rescue his only son from drowning he searched frantically for some way to help his drowning son. He saw a rope laying on the ground, but it had been almost cut in half, as the father grabbed the rope and tossed one end of it to his son. The father yelled to his son," reached beyond the break and hold on."

Although the rope was almost cut in half, the son was able to grab the rope and reach beyond the breaking point and hold on while his father pulled him to safety. Sometimes our faith is just like the rope which the father tossed out to his son, it gets broken and damaged by the situations of life and when we try to use it we see the damage that has been done to it. But we must do as the father instructed his son to do, we must also reach beyond the break and hold on while Jesus pulls us through our demanding situations of life.

When life circumstances cause a break in your faith and you are in an unfavorable situation, you must reach beyond the breaking point of your faith and hold on. I remember when my son passed away from

Colon Cancer at age 19, that tragic situation caused a break in my faith and I found myself drowning in my anger, unanswered questions and doubt. Because I saw my son transformed from 150 pounds of muscle, into 75 pounds of skin and bones. I saw the brilliant light of life in his eyes begin to dim as the end grew near.

I watched my son slowly pass away, and there was nothing that I could do to save him. But I had to reach beyond the break of my faith to hold on, while Jesus pulled me through the most agonizing situation that I had ever faced. I almost let go of the hand of Jesus, I am so happy that he did not let go of me in my weak condition, and I found strength in him. We can always depend on him, because he says in his word that he will never leave us nor forsake us, and he cannot lie.

There's a story of the Barren fig tree in the book of St. Matthew Chapter 21:18 - 22 (NKJV) that reads," now in the morning as he returned to the city, he was hungry. And seeing a fig tree by the road, he came to it and found nothing on it but leaves, and said to it," let no food grow on you ever again." Immediately the fig tree withered away. And when the disciples saw it, they marveled, saying. "How did the tree wither away so soon?" So, Jesus answered and said to them, "assuredly, I say to you. If you have faith and do not doubt, you will not only do what was done to the fig tree, but also if you say to this mountain, be removed and be cast into the sea, it will be done. And whatever things you ask in prayer, believing, you will receive.

What Jesus was saying is that you must reach pass the point of your doubt and hold firmly to what you believe. Because doubt causes a break in your faith and you lose that strong connection with God through Jesus, but when you reach pass your doubt and beyond the break you take hold of the hand of Jesus.When you rely on his strength to pull you through those dire situations, you will realize that no weapon formed against you shall prosper because if he be for you, who or what can be against you? Be encouraged my friends and know that you are never alone. Our God is Omniscient, meaning he knows everything. Our God is Omnipresent, meaning he is present everywhere. Our God is Omnipotent, meaning he has unlimited power and able to do anything. So be encouraged my friends, when situations happen, reach beyond the break and hold on.

Faith that Overcomes Discouragement

WHEN MY PARENTS AND I moved from Leflore County Mississippi to Chicago Illinois, my entire world turned upside down. First, I believe I was in shock because we moved from a first-floor dwelling to the 14th floor of a high-rise apartment building overlooking the Expressway. In Mississippi, we didn't have any buildings that were taller than two stories high and I had never seen or heard of an Expressway, which was a total shock to my senses when I saw it from the 14th floor. I stayed inside for two weeks before I venture out of the apartment, and when my mom did finally take me to school the other kids looked at me as though I was an alien.

Secondly, when my mother enrolled me in school I was so afraid that I hardly talk to anyone, and then one day the teacher called on me to read in front of the class. I sheepishly stood up with my book in my hand that covered my face, and as I began to read all the kids began to laugh at me because I had the worst case of stammering that anyone ever saw. It was the most horrible and humiliating experience as a child that I ever had, I never wanted to go back to school again but my mom had a different plan.

Through the resources of the school my mother was introduced to a speech therapist, who I believe to be my guardian angel in disguise. She was the nicest and kindest lady I had ever met, she had faith in her ability to help me and she had faith in my ability to overcome my stammering problem. She would work with me during school to instill confidence in me, and to remove the low self-esteem that I had for myself. Each time when I felt like giving up she would tell me how strong and smart I was, her words of encouragement and faith made me want to try even harder to overcome my stammering problem.

I looked forward to the sessions with my speech therapist, because she made me feel that my faith was bigger than my fears, and the kids in my room weren't laughing so much anymore. I still had the haters and the teasers that mocked me every time they had the opportunity to do so, but because I had others that believed in me besides my mom I could stand strong against the discouragement of my peers. By the end of the year when I graduated to high school I was totally cured from my stammering problem, my mother was so proud of me and so was my speech therapist. Little did I know, there was more discouragement to come as a teenager and as an adult.

I thank God for a praying mother who instilled her faith in me at an early age, and because of my mother's faith I could believe in my speech therapist, who helped me believe in myself to overcome the discouragement from my peers and to overcome my stammering problem. In the of the book of Nehemiah, Chapter 2:19 (NKJV) says," But when Sanballat the Horonite, Tobiah the Ammonite official, and Geshem the Arab heard of it, they laughed at us and despised us.

There will be times in your life when others can't see what you see, and they try to discourage you and mock you because they don't know your purpose that you have been gifted with. Nehemiah came on the scene and his deep concerned was not for his own well-being, but for the well-being of God's people. Nehemiah's job was to be the cupbearer for the king, he was to select, serve and tastes the king's wine to make sure it was not poisoned. Therefore, the cupbearer had a very important position in the kingdom.

Although he had a very important position with the king, that was not his purpose. God had chosen Nehemiah for a greater purpose, he was chosen to rebuild the wall at Jerusalem and to unite God's people to put aside their petty differences to come together as one body. Nehemiah had to defeat his peers who came to bring discouragement and fear, hoping that he and the Jews would turn away from the purpose that God had called them to. Nehemiah had faith to overcome the discouragement and fear that his enemies tried to inflict upon him.

My friends, had I allowed my peers to discourage me with fear and shame, my mother's prayers and the efforts of my speech therapists would have been in vain, and I would still probably be the stammering mess that I was then. But because of my mother's faith in God, my speech therapist faith in her God given abilities, I had the faith to overcome discouragement. Be encouraged my friends and know that with God nothing is impossible.

Beware of Distractions

HAVE YOU EVER HAD ONE of those nights that you just couldn't sleep? Situations, problems, and other issues going on in your life, and your spirit is telling you that you need to get up and pray and ask for directions, but you make every excuse in the world not to. That situation happened to me and I now have a profound respect for God when He tells me to get up and pray. I've learned that the enemy can cause distractions in your life, and we can also distract ourselves so easily.

Distractions can hinder us and stop God's flow of blessings into our life. Our jobs, our family, our friends, and even our pets can distract us from obeying God. If we would pray when our spirit tells us to pray we could bring about blessings, peace, healings and joy in our lives and the lives of others. I mentioned pets for a reason, because this story is about a little dog name Buddy. Buddy was a mixed breed with a serious under bite, and he was also a great pet and friend.

He would give me that look and tilt his head as though to smile, and I would find myself smiling too. One night I had trouble sleeping, and I felt the need to get up and pray about things that were going on in my life. My spirit really wanted to go and pray but my flesh wanted to stay in bed, my flesh won the fight and I laid in bed a little longer. Again, I felt in my spirit to go and pray but again I ignored it.

The third time the feeling to get up and pray was stronger than before. As I got up to go pray, Buddy met me in the hallway and he went to the back door as though he wanted to go outside. I decided to let him outside before I went to pray, I later learned that was the wrong choice. Buddy ran outside, and I thought he wanted to take care of his business. As I stood in the door waiting for him to finish, I heard him barking and I saw him chasing what I thought was a black cat. I didn't pay it too much attention because our neighbor had a black cat. When I look a little closer I realized it was not a black cat that Buddy was chasing, it was a skunk.

That's when I began to yell for Buddy to come inside, but it was too late. Then I heard it, Buddy begin to yelp because he had gotten sprayed by the skunk. I then ran outside to aid Buddy, and the skunk ran off into the darkness, and I picked up Buddy and ran back into the house. By this time all the commotion has woke up my ex-wife, she's screaming what's going on? What happened to Buddy? Why does it stink in here?

Now I'm trying to explain this whole situation and it's not smelling good or sounding good. We're standing in the laundry room that leads to the back door that goes outside, so I put buddy in the laundry washtub to wash them off. By this time, he is stinky, and I asked my ex-wife what are we going to do? She said," you need to go to the store to get some tomato juice. I said," it's 3:30 in the morning and I stink, and she said," so does Buddy.

So, I go to the store, and lucky for me it was early in the morning and not a lot of people were in the store. So, I picked up the tomato juice and hurried back home, and on my way back home my spirit said," you should have prayed." I get back home and open the tomato juice and we poured it all over Buddy. Our little tan colored dog was now a red smelly angry little dog. Here's the situation. Because I didn't go and pray when I should have, I interrupted the flow of God's blessings on my family.

I should have gone and prayed when I was led to, and none of this would have happened. Every time we are distracted from what we should be doing, we block the flow of blessings. Now I had an angry ex-wife, an angry little red dog, and a smelly house. All because of disobedience, but the story does not end there. I went to work that morning, but when I returned home Buddy had been shaved down to the skin.

I asked my ex-wife why did she shave him so close to the skin? Her answer was that she did not like his red hair, so she decided to cut it with the scissors, but they did not work well. So, she had to use my hair clippers to do the job, and it was a botched-up job. As a result, I had a very angry ex-wife, a bald angry little dog that growls at me when I came close to him, and a smelly house. I really understand now how prayer can change things, if I had only prayed none of those things would've happened to me, or my family or my pet.

As the man in my family it is my responsibility to seek God for direction, guidance, safety, and wellbeing of my family members. It is my duty to make sure that my life is in order, that I may help those in my family learn how to bring order to their lives. It was my disobedience that caused the chaos to happen, because I opened the door that started it all.

In the 28th Chapter of the book of Deuteronomy verses 1-2 (NKJV) it says," now it shall come to pass, if you diligently obey the voice of the Lord your God, to observe carefully all his commandments which I command you today, that the Lord your God was set you high above all the nations of the earth. And all these blessings shall come upon you and overtake you, because you obey the voice of the Lord your God." Blessed shall you be in the city and blessed shall you be in the country." God spelled out to the Israelites very clearly the numerous blessings that would be theirs if they diligently obeyed the voice of the Lord [their] God, to observe carefully His commandments"

(Read Deuteronomy 28) If we want our family to be blessed and not broken, we should obey the voice of the Lord. Matthew 6:33 (NKJV) says," But seek first the kingdom of God and his righteousness, and all these things shall be added to you. Be encouraged my friends.

Beyond What We Can Think or Ask

I HAD A 2001 GMC Yukon truck, I owned this truck for 2 1/2 years and I did not know the capability that the previous owner had equipped this truck with. It had a Kenwood navigational system in the dash, I have used on several occasions the GPS and navigational components, but I never knew of the full capability of this system. I purchased a new smart phone, and I asked my son to connect another device to my smart phone to run it through my radio.

When he had finished I didn't need the device at all that I had asked him to hook up, instead he had everything running on my phone and through the Kenwood navigational system. When I came outside to check on his progress I was blown away by the technology that was available at my requests, and I didn't even know how to use the unlimited capability this system offered. I never knew this system could sync with my smart phone and do everything that my smart phone could do.

He showed me how to make hands-free calls from the navigational system, it had a phonebook that had all my contacts that's on my smart phone. I could send a text message, I could say call John Smith and it dials John Smith number. This device could do far and exceedingly beyond anything I could think or ask of it, I couldn't begin to comprehend all this device could help me accomplish or how it could make my life easier.

I didn't understand the power of technology, but my son showed me that I had this power right at my disposal and I just needed to learn how to access it and utilize it for my own good. One of the good things about this GPS system is that when I make a wrong turn or get lost, it can get me back on track. In like manner but much greater is God, when I was a child my mother taught me how to read the Bible.

She taught me how to pray, believe, and rely upon God, to read his word and it would give directions for my life. His word would lead me out of the darkness into the light, his word would comfort me in my troubles and bring peace during my storms. His word increases my faith, when fear and doubt steps in. Through my weaknesses, I am made strong in him, and in his death, I find my life. I still can't understand why he would give his life for me on the cross, when it should have been me hanging on that tree. He paid a debt that he did not owe, I owe a debt that I could not pay. I don't quite understand the process of salvation, or how His red blood could wash me as white as snow.

I don't understand how he can forgive all my unkind words, my pride, the dumb stuff that I have done throughout my life. I can't quite understand how he loves me despite all my sins, my ungratefulness, my unfaithfulness, my selfishness, my pride, my stinking thinking, (this list could go on forever). He removes my old stony heart, and replaces it with a heart of flesh, and then he showed me how to love others beyond my own capacity.

Ephesians Chapter 3:20 (NKJV) says," now to him who is able to do exceedingly abundantly above all that we ask or think, according to the power that works in us." What God can do in our lives is so intense that it is literally beyond what we can ask or think. The goodness of God goes beyond what our human imagination can conceive. The power that works in us is so strong and immense that we don't completely realize what is happening. His love for us is so total and so strong that he wants the very best for our lives, and he is working to make it happen if we will trust him. Sometimes I have trouble trusting the GPS to get me to my destination, because sometimes it takes me a different route and it makes mistakes.

When you get off track it says," recalculating," rethinking the situation and then it finds the fastest route to get me to my destination. With God, I don't have to worry about him making mistakes, or rethinking the situation, because every way that he takes me is growing and shaping me into what he would have me to be. My GPS takes me to the location that I program into it, and it gets me to my chosen destination; but because of my choosing, it might not be the ideal location for me to grow spiritually or mentally at that time in my life.

On the contrary, when God leads me, and I am open to his will for my life I can grow in every area of my being. The world's GPS, Global Positioning System is an amazing use of technology that has revolutionized travel and brought about major changes in our lives. My GPS, God's Powerful Spirit is (Omnipresent) present everywhere at the same time. (Omnipotent) having unlimited power, able to do anything.

(Omniscient) to know everything there is to know. Therefore, our God can do exceedingly abundantly above all that we ask or think, in Philippians 4:19 (NKJV) it says," and my God shall supply all your needs according to his riches in glory by Christ Jesus." We always worry about money and having our needs met. In fact, we spent all our time and energy in pursuit of security, the believer in

Jesus Christ is to live a life free from the fear of lack of finances or any other thing.

God will take care of our needs through his infinite resources. Seek first the kingdom of God, and his righteousness, and all these things shall be added unto you. Exceedingly and abundantly, be encourage my friends.

Call to be Good Samaritans

LAST WEEK IN PARIS THE example of Good Samaritans was seen on national TV and across the World Wide Web. It was such a blessing to see men lay down their lives for perfect strangers and disregard their own life and safety for the sake of others. Spencer Stone, Alek Skarlatos, Anthony Sadler, heard a shot on the train they on and went to investigate. They saw a man with an AK-47 that was jammed, and the man struggled desperately to get the weapon to fire.

Then Alek tapped Spencer on the shoulder and said Let's go, three Good Samaritans that were ready to go the extra mile for their neighbors, even at risk of their own lives. They were awarded medals of Honor for their heroic deeds, but I believe they have a greater reward in Heaven. I'm reminded of the parable of the Good Samaritan in the book of Luke, Chapter 10:25 -37(NJKV). Here Jesus gives the two greatest commandments, you shall love the Lord your God with all your heart, with all your soul, with all your strength, with all your mind, and your neighbor as yourself.

The man wanting to justify himself, said to Jesus, who is my neighbor? Then Jesus answered and said: A certain man went down from Jerusalem to Jericho, and fell among thieves, who stripped him of his clothing, wounded him, and departed, leaving him half dead. Now by chance a certain priest came down that road and when he saw him, he passed on the other side. Likewise, a Levite and when he arrived at the place, came and looked, and passed by on the other side.

But a certain Samaritan, as he journeyed, came where he was and when he saw him he had compassion on him. So, he went to him and bandaged his wounds, pouring on oil and wine; and he set him on his own animal, brought him to an inn, and took care of him. On the next day, when he departed, he took out two denarii, gave them to the innkeeper, and said to him, take care of him; and whatever more you spend, when I come again, I will repay you.

Which of these three do you think was neighbor to him who fell among the thieves? The man he said," who showed mercy on him." Then Jesus said to him," go and do likewise." The three Good Samaritans on the train fulfill the second greatest commandment. Which is to love your neighbor as yourself. They were willing to lay down their lives for their neighbors, and to disregard their own personal safety. This was truly an act of selflessness, and love for their neighbor as they love themselves.

It is so important to God to break down the barriers of prejudice and hatred which often stands in the way of fulfilling God's two Great Commandments, that we love him and that we love one another. Prejudice is frequently one of hatred's powerful assistants. The Bible makes it clear that in Christ's God sees all people alike and to think otherwise is to be deceived.

When Jesus ministered to the woman of Samaria, he was showing us that the barriers that exist between people, barriers of race, color, social views, economic, gender, and a host of other things people used to separate themselves can be crossed by God's love. Humanity was not originally created to have walls between its members that would prevent people from love and one another. These were introduced by the fall and now can be removed only in Christ. We have the power to love one another. Be encouraged my friends.

Destroying ignorance

PROVERB 4:7 (NKJV) SAYS, "WISDOM is the principal thing, therefore get wisdom: and with all your getting, get understanding." King Solomon, the wisest man in the Bible urges us to get wisdom, because wisdom is the principal thing. He then tells us to get understanding as well. Wisdom is knowing the truth and how to apply it to any given situation, while understanding is knowledge shaped by wisdom and insight. The words wisdom, or wise and understanding occur over 140 times in Proverbs.

The pursuit of knowledge in and of itself produces nothing more than data, which is an accumulation of facts that are useless to us if we do not properly apply them to life situations. Wisdom, then, must be our priority, rather than knowledge, because knowledge without wisdom and understanding is meaningless. Proverb 9:10 (NKJV) tells us," the fear of the Lord is the beginning of wisdom, and the knowledge of the Holy one is understanding." Without a respectful fear and knowledge of the creator of the universe, there is no wisdom or understanding.

Psalms 14:1(NJKV) declares, "the fool has said in his heart, there is no God." The one who fears and reverence the Lord is considered wise, while the one who denies God is a fool. Our attaining of wisdom grows as we draw closer to our Lord; and our relationship with him deepens as we begin to know his nature and his ways. Therefore, revere and honor the Lord, his reproofs, instructions, and advice with humility, knowing that from these come wisdom and understanding.

The results will be patience, discernment, favor, prosperity, and safety. On the contrary, Hosea 4:6 (NKJV) says," my people are destroyed for lack of knowledge. Because you have rejected knowledge, I will also reject you from being priests for me; because you have forgotten the law of your God, I will also forget your children." The children of Israel had rejected God. As a result, there was no truth or mercy or knowledge of God in the land."

When there is no knowledge of God's word or his principles in a society there is social chaos' and destruction. In our day, there is a real lack of knowledge of God in most countries around the world. The result is violence, crime, corruption, and evil in the land. God said," my people are destroyed for lack of knowledge." We destroy ignorance by the pursuit of knowledge, wisdom, and understanding. Knowledge means the accumulation of facts, information, and skills acquired by a person through experience or education.

We in America have experienced thousands of years of victory through prayer and intercession. We know that prayer works, because we have not only heard that it changes people, but we have seen the change in our family member's lives; as well as our own lives. The senseless killings going on in the world today is not something new, it is a continuation of chaos. The Orlando Florida nightclub shooting. The mass shooting in San Bernardino California, the Salt Lake City Utah theater shooting, the Virginia Tech campus shooting, the Sandy Hook elementary school shooting, and the Columbine high school shooting.

It goes on and on, why do we have to wait for another senseless shooting or mass killing before we realize that we need to pray without ceasing, Milwaukee, Chicago, every city in the world is experiencing some form of chaos, and senseless acts of violence. Wisdom teaches us that the heart of man is deceitfully wicked, and his whole nature must be changed. The FBI, the CIA, internal affairs, psychologists, police detectives, Homeland security, every office in government is determining to answer this question.

What caused this individual to go on a shooting spree? What organization were they connected to? This individual had the same problem as all the other individuals that committed similar crimes. They all had their heart harden by sin. Let's examine the knowledge that the Bible gives us about Paul, who was one of the greatest writers in the Bible. Before he became Paul, his name was Saul, and some would say he was a mass murderer because he traveled the land killing Christians for their beliefs.

What is the difference between Saul and Omar Mateen? Saul met Jesus on the road to Damascus, and not only was his name changed but his very nature was changed. Prayer changes people, situations, circumstances, and lives. Therefore, we must pray without ceasing, we all can become intercessors. An intercessor stands in the gap between God and man and prays for the people, the leaders of the city, and the nation. God has given his people in the New Testament the power to intercede for other individuals and for our world.

Sometimes the nation and people are bound by the powers of darkness, we have the divine privilege of praying for them to appropriate the blood of Jesus Christ over their lives and to bind the powers of darkness. It was prayer that caused the heavens to open and rain upon the earth in the days of Elijah. It was prayer that saved Shadrach, Meshach, and Abed-nego from the fiery furnace of Neb-u-chad-nezar.

It was prayer that saved Daniel in the lion's den. In the book entitled the Cross and the Switchblade, it was prayer that changed the heart of Nicky Cruz from a cold-blooded killer, to an evangelist that spreads the good news of the gospel. It was through prayer that Jesus fed the 5000 with five loaves and two fishes. It was through prayer that the mayor of the city invited religious leaders from across the city to come to his office and discuss having prayer to start off every council meeting session.

Only seven religious leaders showed up for the session with the mayor, but they were all thrilled to have an opportunity to be an intercessor for the leaders and their city. Each of us can pray for the nations and its peoples, taking seriously our roles as intercessory prayer warriors and by praying as the Holy Spirit leads. 2 Chronicles 7:14 (NKJV) says," if my people who are called by my name will humble themselves, and pray and seek my face, and turn from their wicked ways, then I will hear from heaven, and will forgive their sin and heal their land."

This is a very important passage on intercessory prayer. It teaches God's people that when there are problems in their nation, communities, families and personal lives, God will heal those situations if they will come to him in humility and repentance. That is if God's conditions are met, which are that we humble ourselves and turn away from our sin, he will hear, forgive our sins, and heal our land. This prayer is of vital importance concerning what is happening in most nations, communities, and homes in the world. Violence, drugs, alcoholism, crime, divorce, sexual perversion, economic problems, poverty, and disease are rampant in our world. However, God's people can do something about it if they humble themselves in prayer and turn from their sin, expecting God to do what only he can do. Be encouraged my friends.

Fear has no power, except that which you give it

FEAR OF FAILURE, FEAR OF man, fear of consequences, fear of moving forward, fear of being lonely, fear of dying, fear of using all your gifts, talents and abilities will keep you crammed in a corner. It's going to take courage and strength beyond your capacity to step out of the box that the world wants to keep you in, because the power of fear will paralyze you and you will remain confined to that box. Charles Spurgeon the great theologian said," the best and wisest thing in the world is to work as if it all depended upon you, and then trust in God, knowing that it all depends upon him."

In my own life fear, doubt and negative self – talk appears daily, and daily I must reinforce faithful and positive thinking to remember who I am and whose I am. Life can be very scary at times, and it can appear that you are stuck between a rock and a hard place with no way out and nowhere to turn. Be honest with yourself, has life situations and circumstances ever made you so afraid that you regretted trying to change your life? Now you want to go back to where you were because it was easier to stay in a tough situation than to try and live in a new situation. Change can be overwhelming, but it can also bring a new beginning if fear is replaced with faith.

I'm reminded of the Red Sea crossing in the 14th chapter of the book of Exodus. There were literally hundreds of thousands of people following Moses out of the land of Egypt, there were men, women and children, young and old, healthy and sick people, some were being carried and some were walking. They left with the dreams and hope of a better life, not knowing where they were going but anywhere was better than Egypt. Cruel taskmasters, being whipped and beaten, forced to make brick without straw, barely enough food or water, any place was better than this place.

Oh, the joy of being delivered from slavery, free at last, free at last, thank God almighty we are free at last. The Red Sea was in the front of them, and on both sides, were hills, and mountains that were impossible for most of the people to pass. None of that mattered now, because they were free, and their dreams were just around the corner. But in the distant the dust from Pharaoh's horses and chariots could be seen. Pharaoh with his great army was coming down on the children of Israel, and the people became afraid as despair shattered their dreams, they panicked in unbelief and said to Moses," is this not the word that we told you in Egypt, saying, let us alone that we may serve the Egyptian?

For it would have been better for us to serve the Egyptians then that we should die in the wilderness. How many of us has allowed fear to shatter our dreams, destroy our hope and made us want to go back and live in the terrible situation that we came out of? The people would rather be slaves in chains and bondage, to be whipped and killed and sold from their families than to die in the wilderness as free men. Fear blinded their eyes and caused them to walk by sight, and not by faith. They preferred their afflictions over faith and freedom, but little did they know that they were about to witness the miraculous.

So, the Egyptians pursued them, all the horses and chariots of Pharaoh, and overtook them camping by the sea and Pi Hahiroth, before Baal Zephon. They were very afraid, and they cried out to Moses. And Moses said to the people, do not be afraid. Stand still and see the salvation of the Lord which He will accomplish for you today. When we replace fear with faith, our whole world changes because fear is dethroned, and faith is victorious. God told Moses to tell the people to go forward, fear can only stop you when you have no determination. God wants His people to go forward, not to the left nor the right but forward. We build up walls that God wants to tear down, fears that God must eradicate.

Instead of us telling God how big our storms and fears are, we should tell our storms and fears how big our God is. Fear, doubt, and unbelief closed the people in, but one man's unshakable faith opened the Red Sea and the children of Israel walk through on dry land. God has already made provision for our victory also, but fear will cause the people to look down when they should be looking up.

Fear causes us to take our eyes off God and look to ourselves, God knows how to run our lives better than we do. Jeremiah 29:11 (NJKV) says," for I know the thoughts that I think toward you, says the Lord, thoughts of peace and not of evil, to give you a future and a hope." God has assured your victory, do not allow fear to paralyze you in your tracks and stop you from moving forward. Fear has no power except that which we give it, God has not given us a spirit of fear, but of power, and of love, and a sound mind. Be encouraged my friends, change your mind, change your life.

Hardhearted

DR. TONY EVANS RELATES THIS story. A man was in prison and in need of some money. He wrote his mother and asked her to send $500 immediately. Soon after, he got a package in the mail. It was a Bible. On the top of the Bible, there was a letter that said, "Son, I love you. Pray and read your Bible." The man was ticked off. He got on the phone and called his mother. "Mama, I appreciate the Bible, but what I need right now is $500. She told him over the phone, "Son, pray and read your Bible."

He got more ticked off and hung up on his mother. He then wrote a letter. "Mother, I know you believe in God, but that's the problem with you Christians. You are so heavenly minded that you don't know how to function in the real world. What I need is $500, I don't need a Bible. I need a check or five $100-dollar bills! If I need money, don't send me a Bible and tell me to pray!" He got a letter back that said, "Son, pray and read your Bible." He was so irritated at his mother, that for the six months he was in jail that Bible stayed in the corner.

After a long while, he finally got out. His mother was there to meet him. He could hardly speak to her. Mama, you let me down, I needed you as my mother and you let me down. She said," what do you mean son"? I wrote you, I called you, I begged you for $500 and every time you gave me this same old line to pray and read my Bible.

Well son, did you pray and read your Bible? Yeah, I prayed and read my Bible and I'm still as broke as I was when you told me the first time to pray and read my Bible.

Son, do you have your Bible?" He reached in his bag and he handed her the book. Son, let me ask you one more time. Did you pray and read your Bible? Yes, Mama, I told you I prayed and read my Bible. Son, you neither prayed nor read your Bible. She opened the Bible and at every major divisional section within the text, there was a $100 bill taped inside of it. If the boy would have read his Bible, he would have understood that the thing he was looking for was in the text.

Because he didn't take seriously the word of God, what the word of God had to offer he never received. Many of our youth of today is of that same mindset. They are hard, angry, and disrespectful. The Rapper Fat Joe was asked, "Why are our young men so angry?" His reply was, because everyone wants to be hard. Our young people have hardened their hearts, but hardened heart cannot receive the blessings of God.

In the book of Jeremiah, Chapter 4:3 (NJKV) says," For thus says the Lord to the men of Judah and Jerusalem, breakup your follow ground and sow not among thorns." The word fallow means uncultivated or untilled land. The 13th chapter of Matthew talks about the condition in which one should sow seed to reap a harvest. A farmer must first cultivate his land, and sow seed into good ground before he can reap the harvest. Likewise, God must cultivate our hearts to be prepared to receive our blessings.

Only God can renew our heart. In the book of Ezekiel, 36:26 (NKJV) says," A new heart also will I give you, and a new spirit will I put within you: and I will take away the stony heart out of your flesh, and I will give you a heart of flesh." Just like the young man in the story, our situations, surroundings, and our circumstances can sometimes make us hard and callous. And we refused to hear instructions from those who love us. But also, like the mother in the story said, "Pray and read your Bible."

That must also be the message that we give to the people we love. We must break up the fallow ground of our heart, if we are to change and receive God's blessings that he has in store for us. Because preparation precedes blessings, 2 Kings 3:16-17(NKJV) says," no water was given for the Army until the ditches were dug. Hosea 10:12 (NKJV) says, "No harvest until the ground had been broken up." Had the young man in our story prayed and read his Bible, his circumstances would have been changed dramatically. Back in the day, the old people used to say that a child was hardheaded.

Now our youth are hardhearted, one can change the thoughts that are in our head. But it takes God to change the conditions of the heart. One of the greatest kings in the Bible needed God to change his heart. King David said in Psalm 51:10 (NKJV)," Create in me a clean heart O God; and renew a right spirit within me." We need God to work this identical process in us and our children today, because just like King David we all have gone astray, but we all can come back and be totally changed and be a blessing to those around us.

Never stop praying for those you love, they will return home someday. I thank God for my mother, through her prayers God brought me back from the brink of destruction when I broke up the fallow ground of my heart. He can do the same for you and your children, be encouraged my friends.

Hidden Treasure Inside

AS I OPENED THE DOOR I was greeted by fear and he asked me," for what are you looking? I replied," am looking for the gifts, talents and abilities that once lived here." Fear said," there is nothing here except broken dreams, failed plans, unrealized potential, nothing of value. Please go now, because what you seek is not here, but I replied," I know they once lived here because I remember this place.

But fear replied strongly, you must have been mistaken or you have the wrong address; as he tried to close the door. I will not leave because I know that they are here, and I have come back to release them from this dark place where you have imprisoned them. Fear began to shout," you must leave this place now or you will be sorry you ever came back here." So, you do remember me, never the less I have returned for all my gifts, that you stole from me; they must live so that I can live and fulfill my destiny.

As fear ran away screaming," it's not over, I will return, and you will be sorry." I began to understand that I had given all my power over to fear, but now I realized the potential that God had given me to do great exploits. Have you also succumbed to the empty threats of fear? Has it caused you to abandon your hopes, dreams, and a larger vision for your life? Has fear caused you to walk away from your dreams? What ideas, plans, and goals have you seen as possible, but fear caused you walk by sight and not by faith?

When you believe what fear says instead of what God says for your life, you will always be afraid and abandon the vision that God has given you for your life. Fear tells you that your dreams are impossible and remind you of all the times you failed. God tells you that nothing will be impossible to him who believes. Fear says," you didn't finish high school, you didn't go to college; you are not as smart as everyone else. God said in Isaiah 41:10 (NKJV)," fear not, for I am with you, be not dismayed, for I am your God, I will strengthen you, yes, I will help you, yes, I will uphold you with the right hand of my righteousness."

Fear says," you won't be a success or do great things. Daniel said in Chapter 11:32b (NKJV)," but the people who know their God shall be strong and carry out great exploits." Fear says," you have nothing to offer the world, you are small and insignificant." God said in first Corinthians1:27 (NKJV)," but God has chosen the foolish things of the world to confound the wise; and God has chosen the weak things of the world to confound the things which are mighty." Do you know that you have the potential to make this world a better place?

You have the potential to make someone a better person, you have the potential to offer solutions for the world's problems. Fear of failure, fear of man, and fear of consequences will keep you crammed in a corner. It's going to take courage for you to step out of the box that the world wants to put you in and take your seats in the first-class section of life. The great theologian Charles Spurgeon said," the best and wisest thing in the world is to work as if it all depended upon you, and then trust in God, knowing that it all depends on him."

God has given us the power to overcome fear and every other enemy of our potential, but we must access that power to be successful in our personal lives, in our family, and in our homes. Author, speaker, and late Pastor Dr. Myles Munroe said in his book Maximizing Your Potential," Tragedy strikes when success dies in failure, hope dies in despair, and vision dies in the absence of confidence." If we are living in fear, despair, and unbelief we must go and take back what the enemy of fear has stolen from us.

We cannot live in a place that is absent of confidence, but that confidence cannot be in ourselves it must be in the power of God working through us. Second Corinthians 4:7 (NKJV) says," but we have this treasure in earthen vessels, that the excellence of the power may be of God and not of us." Such wonderful treasures are laid up inside of us, but it takes the power of God to access it and bring it to the surface that it can make a difference in the world, our families, our homes, and in our personal lives.

We have these treasures that are waiting to be discovered, that can bring such richness and purpose to our lives and that of others. But we must go to the enemy's camp and take back what he stole from us. Then, we can make our lives better for our children, and our families that God has given us. Oh yes, fear did return, but only to be defeated again. Yes, I did take back my gifts, talents, and abilities that had been given to me by God to fulfill His purpose. To make a significant contribution to my family, and to the lives of others. Never again will I relinquish my power and potential to fear or any other enemy. My favorite book says," to whom much has been given, much is required."

We have been given such a great treasure, and we must protect it at all costs, the enemy knows if he steals our treasure we have nothing of value to help our family and our fellow man. Do not allow fear to rob you of your gifts, for you have greatness inside of you that can help your family, and the world. Be encouraged my friends.

Light in darkness

MY FRIEND AND I DROVE to Mississippi on September 28th, 2015. She wanted to walk across the Edmund Pettis Bridge in Selma Alabama for her 50th birthday to commemorate Bloody Sunday. Plus, I wanted to see relatives in Mississippi that I had not seen in 40 years, so we both were equally excited to make the trip. As we made our way through the south and seeing the cotton fields and dusty roads brought back a flood of memories of my childhood.

I visited aunts and cousins that I had not seen since I was a teenager, they pulled out picture albums of days gone by and told stories that I had long forgotten. I was very embarrassed by some of the stories that were told to my friend by my cousins about things I did as a child. If you know southern people, you know everyone has a nickname. So, please forgive me if I do not mention my nickname, I'm in my mid-life and they still call me by my nickname; how embarrassing. I shared with my friend the story of how I had to go and get water from the well at night.

I had a dog that was a shepherd and collie mixed, he was quite a big dog and I named him big track. Mainly because he was a big dog with big feet that made big tracks, so I called him big track. At night, when I had to go to the well to get a bucket of water I would take big track with me. I was afraid of the dark and I hated going to the well by myself because it was so dark. My mother was the greatest cook in the world, and big track and I loved her biscuits.

I would save two biscuits and I would break off small pieces of the biscuits and give it to big track all the way to the well and back to the house. It was so dark between our house and the well that it would literally make the hairs on the back of my neck stand up. My imagination created things like a one eye, three horns, people eating monster. I thought the bogeyman lived in the darkness between our house and the well. Big track was my savior and protector from the monsters in the dark. Big track died, I grew up and we moved away to Chicago.

End of story, my friend enjoyed the stories of my childhood and thought they were funny. But I remained afraid of the darkness until my mid-30s. When I found out that my childhood imaginary problems had turned into adult spiritual problems. At this age, I was still afraid of the monsters in the dark, but this was not physical darkness anymore, this was spiritual darkness. I didn't have my dog big track to protect me and to walk with me through this spiritual darkness.

There were situations, circumstances, fears, doubts, shame, loneliness, hopelessness, poverty and a host of other physical and spiritual hurdles that I had to jump over in life. It gets very scary walking in the dark with no light for your path, or to guide your footsteps. I can remember the times when I left home and did not leave a light on, and when I came back home it was dark in the house and I stumbled over furniture and things on the floor while trying to get to the light switch.

But when I turned on the light there was no stumbling over anything and I was not afraid. I knew that I needed light to chase the darkness away so that I would not be afraid to live my life to my full potential. This brings me to what I want to say, I have found the light of life, or should I say the light of life found me, and I no longer walk in darkness nor am I afraid. I walk in confidence now, not my own confidence but in the confidence of knowing Jesus as my Lord and Savior. Psalm 119:105 (NKJV) says," your word is a lamp unto my feet and a light to my path."

To me, that means that I will never have to walk in spiritual darkness again. I will never have to be afraid of things in the dark that I don't understand, because His word brings light to the situations and circumstances that occur in my life. By the way, my friend and I did walk across the Edmund Pettis Bridge in Selma Alabama. We thanked God for all those brave souls that crossed that bridge on that terrible day. We have so much to be thankful for in all aspects of our lives, do you have any bridges that you need to cross? Be encouraged my friends, there's no time like today.

Negative self-talk kill dreams

HE HAD THE GIFTS, TALENTS, and abilities, but he always told himself that he was not smart enough. He did not have the inspiration, motivation or the positive attitude to believe that he could be a success. All his close friends could see the tremendous potential that was so obvious and alive within him. He had surrounded himself with the right group of people, but his mind was still full of fear, doubt, and negative self-talk about himself.

It was that internal voice inside his head that kept him from accomplishing his dreams and living up to his full potential. Dr. Myles Monroe said," Tragedy strikes when success dies in failure, when hope dies in despair, and when vision dies in the absence of confidence.

Although his friends were constantly in his ear with words of encouragement, they could not penetrate the wall of negative self-talk that he had erected through fear and doubt. How many dreams, inventions, songs, ideas, and plans have succumbed to the power of fear, doubt, and negative self-talk? The graveyard is full of what could have been, what should have been, what would have been, had it not been for fear, doubt and negative self-talk.

Negative self-talk about ourselves and others keep us from seeing the many benefits that we could add to other lives, but especially our own. Negative self-talk build walls and over time they become fortified and impenetrable. They cannot be broken down from the outside; they must be broken from the inside. In other words, you must initiate the process by eradicating your fears, doubts, and negative self-talk.

True story, after being married for many years and suddenly finding myself in divorce court, fear, doubt, shame, and of course negative self-talk were all present and accounted for. Just for fun depression and anger came along for the ride. I felt myself heading for self-destruction. All I had going for me was my faith, so I began to pray very specific prayers. Although I did not feel any different I believed that things would change. But I had to be opened to new situations.

A close friend invited me to his wife's birthday party; I really had no interest in going or talking to anyone. But out of respect for him and our friendship, reluctantly I attended the party. All my new acquaintances came with me, fear, doubt, shame, and of course negative self-talk. They followed me all around the party everywhere I went, even to the bathroom. O yeah, Shame brought his cousin whose was name was Loneliness, I really disliked that guy.

Then I saw the most beautiful woman in the world, and I knew it was my destiny to be there. The moment I set my mind on her fear, doubt, and shame and of course negative self-talk started a very negative conversation all by them without my approval. There was a literal battle going on inside of my head. Loneliness was threatening to hold me captive forever; Shame spoke of the embarrassment and disgrace that I had caused. Fear made me apprehensive about my future, and doubt begins to destroy my confidence.

Negative self-talk ate away at everything else that was left, but they could not destroy my faith, and my faith was the defensive weapon that brought about the annihilation of the negative self-talk family. When negative self-talk died, fear jumped out of the window, doubt dug his own grave and covered himself up, shame committed suicide, loneliness changed his identity to live and love. After fear jumped out of the window, he didn't go far, he stood between my pass and my future.

I chose to step across the line of fear into my destiny and a new beginning. My life has been transformed because I annihilated the negative self-talk family. I now walk with a new family, they are purpose, passion, potential, and positive self-talk. They are truly my friends, and they tell me of great things that are in store for me. Positive self-talk tells me that nothing is impossible.

My life was changed because I changed my thoughts, my thoughts changed my behavior, my behavior created new opportunities, new opportunities led me to bigger and better things, bigger and better things revealed my purpose, my purpose revealed my passion, my passion revealed my potential, my potential revealed that there is a plan for my life. We have not received a spirit of fear, but of power, and love, and a sound mind. Be encouraged my friends.

Never alone

I AM SURE YOU HAVE heard or read Margaret Rose Powers," Footprints in the Sand. "The words bring such clarity to the phrase," never alone. The Poem talks about her walking along beside God, but in her lowest times she only saw one set of footprints. 2nd Corinthians 5:7 (NKJV) says," We walk by faith, and not by sight." How many times have we did the exact same thing that she did? We walked according to what we saw, and we let our eyes guide our heart, instead of faith guiding our heart. So many times when we can't see or feel God, the enemy will try and make us think that we are alone. Deuteronomy 31:6 (NKJV) says," Be strong and of good courage, do not fear nor be afraid of them; for the Lord your God, He is the one that goes with you. He will not leave you nor forsake you

In the book of Joshua, the phrase," do not be afraid God is with you," spoke to the heart of Joshua and encouraged him. When the Lord called Joshua to lead the people into battle for the promised land, Joshua was understandably scared; but the Lord reminded him, "Do not be afraid, nor be dismayed, for the Lord your God is with you." Joshua chose to believe and obey the promise of God, and he embarked on an astounding 25-year adventure. He saw the river waters part, walls crumble, the sun stands still, and 31 kingdoms conquered, just to mention a few! Joshua depended upon God's power and gave him the glory for every victory.

He found that real courage was trusting in God, full maturity in surrendering to God, wise leadership in following God, and true obedience was through a heart of love for God. The Lord still looks to do great things through servants with hearts like Joshua's. Do you find yourself alone and afraid sometimes, with your children and grandchildren all grown and gone out in the world to start their own lives? Does the condition of the world and the plight of the people cause you to fear for your safety?

Does the rise in healthcare and prescription drugs, economics, global warming, the loss of friends, family, loved ones, and of course your own mortality that causes you to be afraid? Remember in one of the paragraphs she said," during the most troublesome time in my life there was only one set of footprints." Do you remember the Lord's reply? He said," When you saw only one set of footprints, it was then that I carried you." It is so calming and assuring to know that during our times of trials and suffering we are being carry through these situations in his strength and not our own.

When my mother passed away at age 44, when my son passed away at age 19, when my great grandson passed away at age 2, when the doctor gave me the bad news that I had cancer, and when my wife left me, I was never alone because he carried me during those times which were the lowest points in my life. Have there ever been times in your life when you felt like everyone had abandoned you? God carried me through my lowest points, and he will carry you through yours also.

In the book of Joshua in the first verse, God tells Joshua Moses' assistant that his servant Moses is dead and that he will lead the people over the river Jordan. Joshua 1:5 (NKJ) say," no man shall be able to stand before you all the days of your life; as I was with Moses, so I will be with you. I will not leave you nor for sake you." There have been leaders and trailblazers in your life, that mentored you, corrected you, and showed you the right way to live.

Maybe they have gone on to be with the Lord, and now it's your turn to step up and be the leader and trailblazer for your family. You must be strong and of good courage and be not afraid of the battles that lie ahead of you. We do not know what tomorrow holds, but we do know who holds tomorrow in the palm of his hand. When the night gets the darkness, and the day gets the longest, when your strength is depleted, and you stand facing the storms of life, you must remember you are not alone.

There is one who stands beside you who commands the wind, He holds back the rain, he shelters you from the storm; he says peace be still and the storm must obey. He whispers gently and lovingly into your spirit," my precious, precious child, I love you and I will never, never leave you nor forsake you." Be encouraged my friends, God loves you and He is standing and waiting with open arms.

No vacancies

LUKE 2:7 (NKJV) SAYS," AND she brought forth her firstborn son, and wrapped him in swaddling clothes, and laid him in a manger, because there was no room for them in the inn. There was no room in the inn for Joseph, Mary, and Jesus; and so, they stayed in a stable. Then Jesus was wrapped in swaddling clothes, which were long strips of cloth used to wrap infants; and he was placed in a manger. A manger is the feeding trough for livestock, which in this case was filled with hay and doubled as a cradle.

The fact that there was no room in the Inn can be seen to symbolize that sinful mankind has no place for Jesus Christ in their lives. The very God of the universe was not welcome on earth! How sad it is that our lives are so full of unnecessary clutter that we do not have room in our lives for the very God of the universe. As I look at the condition of the world, the broken families, homes, lives, and children, I see such a need for the Savior to come into our lives and do a new thing that will revolutionize our thinking and living.

We make room in our lives for things that make no sense, add no value, and bring no lasting joy to our situations; yet we refuse to allow the Prince of Peace, the King of Kings, the Lord of Lords into our lives that can bring a change to our mind, heart, and spirit. King David had filled his heart with sinful lust and even murder, but he asked God to create within him a clean heart and renew within him unclean spirit and God did.

I realize that everyone is not a Christian, but I also understand that if I have something or know of a tool or a technique that can change one's life, I should be willing to share that with whoever is in need and whosoever will listen. My job is to tell others what I've come through and the experience that has changed my life, and my way of living. Peering into the broken homes and lives of inner-city families, I see the hopelessness, frustration, and despair that chokes the very life out of the families that are living in a sea of poverty and violence.

Young men that walk the streets of the city with no job, no education, and no life skills to prepare them for a productive future. They carry $600 smart phones and they text people instead of talking to people; and in their home, they have 50-inch Smart TV's that is equipped with the latest X box and every gaming device that is available. They walk around in $200 Jordan gym shoes and apparel, and their lives are filled with baby mama drama.

Young women walking around looking for love in all the wrong places, hoping to find value and love in some young man's heart; thinking that if she gives him a child he will love her even more. We all make room in our lives for unnecessary pain, failure, and disappointments; rather than for life, love, and fulfillment of purpose. There is a story in the Bible about a demon possessed man that was healed when he made room in his heart for Jesus Christ.

Luke 8:26 (NKJV) talks about when Jesus and his disciples sailed to another country. It reads," When he stepped out on the boat onto the shore there he met a certain man from the city who had demons for a long time, and he wore no clothing and he did not live in a house but in the tombs. When he saw Jesus, he cried out and felled down before him and with a loud voice he said," what have I to do with you, Jesus Son of the Most High God?

I beg you, do not torment me! For he had commanded the unclean spirit to come out of the man for it had often seized him, that he was kept under guard, bound with chains and shackles; and he broke the bonds and was driven by the demon into the wilderness. Jesus asked him, what is your name? And he said Legion," because many demons had entered him. He begged him that he would not command them to go out into the abyss.

Now a herd of swine was feeding there on the mountain. So, they begged him that he would permit them to enter the swine's, and he permitted them. Then the demons went out of the man and entered the swine's, and the herd ran violently down the steep place into the lake and drown. When those who fed them saw what had happened, they ran and told it in the city and in the country.

Then they went out to see what had happened, and came to Jesus, and found the man from whom the demons had departed, sitting at the feet of Jesus, clothed and in his right mind. When we make room for Jesus in our hearts, mind, and spirit, we also can be unchained, unshackled, and set free. There are many people in this world that is in the same situation as this demon possessed man, who was under guard, bound with chains and shackles.

Demonic possession and oppression by the powers of darkness always results in people being bound and shackled spiritually. In our present day, people have filled their lives with addiction, lust, anger, violence, pride, fear, doubt, perversion, the occult, and so much more, and they are bound just as this man was. Jesus set this man freed through the power of the spirit. That same Holy Ghost Spirit is available to set us free today and break every chain that binds us.

But you my friend, must make room in your heart for the only one that can change your life and the lives of those you love. Will you make room today in your heart? Remember, there is power to break every chain, to break every chain that binds you or your love ones. My Friend, be encouraged.

Parents are leading, even when they are absent.

HAVE WE FAILED OUR YOUNG men and women? Have we led them to believe that there is no hope for their future? Have we caused them to have no regard for life or the laws of this land? Have we caused them to live recklessly, to disregard life and act irresponsibly? Have we caused them to cast their moral conscience so far away that it is irretrievable? Is the condition of our young people our fault (the parents) or theirs (society)?

I would like to say that it is ours fault, parents, grandparents, people who say they love these children. After all, the apple doesn't fall too far from the tree, and we who care for them and provide for them should be teaching them right from wrong. Or should I say, teaching them that they are right and everyone else is wrong. Teaching them to respect others, or should I say, teaching them to have no respect for others, remembering the fact that my child is a mini-me, so what I put in I get out.

We have been instructed to direct our children in the right way, you know, to train up a child; but in some cases, the train has run off the track. I ask you" when did we let go of the wheel? Who was driving the train? Was it someone with a learner's permit or someone with an invalid operator's license? Or was it someone with a need for speed that was high on all the wrong things and unable to see the danger signs and the warning lights?

Have we closed our eyes to the problems that we have created? While we try to shift the blame to others for the fire in our homes that we allow to burn out of control, and out of control it is. More prisons are being built, more homes are fatherless; more laws are being written to take away parental rights. More drugs are entering our neighborhoods, more young men and women are being lost in the system, and more young women are having babies at an alarming rate.

I read that if the blind leads the blind, then they both fall into a ditch. If no one is willing to lead our young people, then who will they follow? The parent is the child's first teacher, that parent is leading in a positive or negative way even if they say nothing. I read a poem once that was quoted by John Maxwell, it was called "The Little Chap Who Follows Me," A careful man I want to be, A little fellow follows me; I do not dare go astray, for fear he'll go the self-same way.

Our children are following in our footsteps, and the problem is that we went the wrong way and now they are going the wrong way also. It's time to redirect our steps and correct our mistakes, it's time for men to come back home, not just to an address but to God's morals and values, to mothers and children, to church and communities.

Whether we realize it or not we are leading our children, even in our absence we are leading them. 89% of what a child learns comes through visual stimulation, 10% through audible stimulation, and 1% through other senses. So, it makes sense that the more children see and hear their parents being consistent in actions and words, the greater their consistency and loyalty. What they hear, they understand; and what they see, they believe. Somewhere during finding ourselves, we lost something.

Billy Graham said," If we lose money, we lose nothing; if we lose health, we lose something, but if we lose character and integrity, we lose everything." I say to you my friend, you have greatness inside of you; your children have the same stuff within them. But someone must show them how to access it, you are the chosen one and you must show them the way. Be encouraged, be strong, be bold for your family, and take the lead, lead on.

Power to break every chain

IT'S BEEN OVER 20 YEARS since I stopped smoking cigarettes, and I have never felt better in my life. As the world becomes more health conscious, I see people struggling with this addiction now more than ever. Not only nicotine addiction, but also drugs and alcohol are plaguing our homes, our families, and our lives. According to the American Cancer Society about 42 million people (somewhat fewer than 1 in 5) adults currently smoke cigarettes.

Tobacco use does not end with cigarettes: other forms of tobacco use are common. In 2013, a survey by the US: (Substance Abuse and Mental Health Administration) reported that 13.4 million people smoked cigars, and 2.5 million people smoked tobacco in pipes. The same survey reported 9 million people use smokeless or spit tobacco.

Tobacco use, including smoking cigarettes, cigars, e- cigarettes, and hookahs, (a hookah is an Oriental tobacco pipe with a long, flexible tube that draws the smoke through water contained in a bowl), as well as using chew or spit tobacco such as snus and snuff, is common among American youth, according to the most recent government surveys.

Despite declines in recent years, and 2012 nearly 1 in 4 male high school students (23%) and nearly 1 in 5 female high school students (18%) were found to be current users of some type of tobacco. Nearly

1 in 7 students (14%) were considered current cigarette smokers. Typically, about half of the students reported that they've tried to quit smoking during the past year. Cigar smoking was also common among high school students, (about 8% of females and 17% of males).

Even though flavorings are no longer allowed in cigarettes, "little cigars" (which often look like brown cigarettes) are sold in candy fruit flavors that appeal to youth. Also, in 2012, about 7% of middle school students use some form of tobacco, with cigarettes (nearly 4%) being the most common. Almost 3% had smoke cigars. In both middle school and high school, tobacco use was higher among male students for all products.

Behavioral problems have also been linked to smoking. Studies have shown that students who smoke are also more likely to use other drugs, get in fights, carry weapons, try to kill themselves, and take part in risky sex. According to the (NCADD), National Council on Alcoholism and Drug Dependence Inc. more than half of all adults have a family history of alcoholism or problem drinking, and more than 7 million children live in a household where at least one parent is dependent on or has abused alcohol.

Alcohol abuse and alcoholism can affect all aspects of a person's life. Long term alcohol use can cause serious health complications, can damage emotional stability, finances, career, and impact one's family, friends and community. Our children and family members, and our community do not have to suffer in vain. There is help.

There is power to break every chain, every bondage, every addiction, every problem, every circumstance, every hopeless situation, every life that is in disarray, every shattered dream, every home that is in shambles, there is power to break every chain that holds you in bondage. My mother showed me where the power was, and how to access that power.

But like most young people I was hardheaded, and I almost destroyed my life before I realized that I had to make a choice. In the Book of Joshua, 24:15 (NKJV) Joshua says to the people, "And if it seems evil to you to serve the Lord, choose for yourself this day whom you will serve, whether the gods which your fathers served that were on the other side of the river, or the gods of the Amorites, in whose land you dwell. But as for me and my house, we will serve the Lord."

Joshua knew and remembered the victories he had won through the power of the Lord. Like Joshua I want my children and my family to be successful, not afraid, not living in bondage to any situation. So, it is my duty to teach them what has been given to them, and that there is power to break every chain and to live a victorious life. Second Timothy 1:7 (NKJV) says," for God has not given us the spirit of fear; but of power, and of love, and of a sound mind." There is power to break every chain, I know where the power is, it is in Jesus Christ my Lord. Be encouraged.

Solid rock or sinking sand

The House on the Rock is a tourist attraction located between the cities of Dodgeville and Spring Green, Wisconsin. Opened in 1959, it is a complex of architecturally unique rooms, streets, gardens, and shops designed by Alex Jordan, Jr. The House on the Rock is a fascinating place, and you must see it to believe it. How on earth this artist could conceive such a plan and bring it to life is beyond me, but I believe it is the perfect example to use with what I'm about to tell you.

Matthew 7:24 - 25 (NKJV) says," Therefore whoever hears these sayings of mine, and does them, I will liken him to a wise man who built his house on the rock. And the rain descended, the floods came, and the winds blew and beat on that house; and it did not fall, for it was founded on a rock." The house on the rock was designed in 1959, and it has stood for 57 years.

During that 57 years' hundreds of storms have beat up on that house, and yet it continues to stand because it was built on a rock. How many storms have your house been through, and is it still standing strong? Let's talk about real storms in our lives that are meant to test our foundation, like dealing with the difficult or broken relationship. Going through a fiscal crisis, withstanding legal problems, unpleasant or painful health problems, the death of someone you love.

Dealing with rebellious children, facing something that brought public disgrace, being laid off from work, or dealing with drug or alcohol problems. The storms of life will come but if the house is built up on a rock, no matter what the problems are the house will stand. That rock is Jesus Christ, and no matter what storm comes your way, you will be able to withstand any storm because your house is built upon the rock.

I remember the storms in Mississippi that would cause my father to leave my mother and I in the house alone while he ran and hid under a bridge from the storm. While he hid from the storm under the bridge, my mother and I hid away from the storm in the arms of Jesus. My mother would call me to her side and we would set in this big rocking chair in the back room, and my mother would rock and pray with me in her lap all throughout the storm.

Sometimes the thunder would seem so loud, that I thought it was in the same room with us. I never understood why my father ran and left us alone, nor why he was so afraid of storms. But it was one thing that I did know, that Jesus Christ was the rock that my mother built her house up on. My mother taught me that Jesus can bring peace in the mist of any storm that I will ever go through.

Uncertainty is around every corner, but one thing is certain, Jesus said I will never leave you nor forsake you. In him we stand and whether any storm. Look at the number of families that have been destroyed by divorce, fatherlessness, violence, alcohol and drug abuse. Our young people are committing suicide through cyber bullying, negative thinking, and no foundation to build on. Some people seem to have it all in life, money, power and fame; but still their lives come crashing down. Only Jesus Christ and the reality of God's word offers complete security in this world.

People who build their lives on anything other than this solid foundation will find that when the winds of change come, as they often do in life, their lives fall apart. For example, if we build our lives on anything that can be taken from us like our looks, popularity, first string on the varsity squad, a relationship, money, or a job, then we will be insecure. An individual can only get so many face lifts, no matter how popular you are someone is going to dislike you for whatever reason. Praise God that Christ cannot be taken from us, nor can we be snatched out of his hand, nor will He ever leave us or forsake us!

That is true personal security. Friends, whatever storms that are raging in your life at this time did not come to stay, they came to pass. If your house is built upon the rock, you have a solid foundation that cannot be shaken by the storms of life. So, let the rains come, and the winds blow, and let them beat upon the house: but it will not fall, because it is built upon the rock, Jesus Christ. Until next time, be encouraged.

Thanksgiving brings thanks-full living

COUNT YOUR MANY BLESSINGS, NAME them one by one, count your many blessings and see what God has done. Have you ever actually counted your many blessings? As I look back over my life and consider all the times that God has blessed me, and did so many wonderful things in my life, I have to say thank you Lord.

I realize that I have so much to be thankful for, I could've been dead, I could've been in prison, I could've been strung out on drugs, I could've been homeless, I could've been living in poverty, I could be without a job, I could've been born with a birth defect, and the list could go on and on. So now I choose to stop and reflect over my life and say thank you, for all that you brought me through.

Growing up in the mean streets of Chicago with gangs, drugs and violence on all sides of me, put me in danger of losing my life every day. I could've have been in the middle of a gang war and got shot up, but He protected me and I thank God that He protected me in my youth and kept me out of harm's way, in all my foolishness and stinking thinking he shielded me from the blast.

I choose to look back over my life with an attitude of gratitude, because Pastor Harris was not always the person that you see and know now. I am grateful for His strength, because I know of my weaknesses. I am grateful for the peace that's in my life now, because I know the storms that He brought me through. I am grateful for the valleys in my life, because I remember the mountains that He brought me over. I am grateful for the sunshine in my life, because I remember the dark days that He brought me out of.

I am thankful for the food that He gave me, because I remember many days being hungry. I am thankful for the joy that I now have in my life, because I remember the sorrow and pain that life inflicted me with. I am thankful for the friends and family He placed around me, because I remember the agony of being so lonely. I am thankful that he did not condemn me for my sins, because I remember being guilty of every one of them. I am thankful that he did not give me a spirit of fear, but of power, love, and a sound mind.

Psalm 95:2 (NKJV) says," Let us come before His presence with thanksgiving." Thanksgiving, todah (toh-dah): the word "thanksgiving" means far more than just sitting down to eat a turkey dinner. Thanksgiving is a powerful spiritual principle. The Psalmist wrote: "Let us come before God's presence with thanksgiving." When we give thanks to God, we are both honoring and worshiping Him as God. God delights in hearing our Thanksgiving in the same way an earthly father is pleased to hear his own children expressions of gratitude for his goodness to them.

I read a quote the other day on thankfulness, "it said each day I am thankful for the nights that turned into mornings, friends that turned into family, dreams that turned into reality, and likes that turned into love."

Here are some quotes on thankfulness that I have read and found heartwarming.

"Be thankful for what you have; you'll end up having more. If you concentrate on what you don't have, you will never, ever have enough"

— Oprah Winfrey

Whatever happens in your life, no matter how troubling things might seem, do not enter the neighborhood of despair.

Even when all doors remain closed, God will open a new path only for you. Be thankful!"

— Elif Shafak, The Forty Rules of Love

"Perhaps it takes a purer faith to praise God for unrealized blessings than for those we once enjoyed or those we enjoy now."

— A.W. Tozer

"Those blessings are sweetest that are won with prayer and worn with thanks."

— Thomas Goodwin

We would worry less if we praised more. Thanksgiving is the enemy of discontent and dissatisfaction."

— H.A. Ironside

What a true statement that H.A. Ironsides just quoted," we would worry less if we praised more. Friends we have so much to praise God for, and to thank him for all that he is done in our lives. Would you take the challenge? Count your many blessings, name them one by one, count your many blessings, and see what God has done. Sometimes we can get so bogged down in day to day activities, and we become so busy that we forget the lesson that was learned in elementary school.

Stop, look, and listen. Take time to look at where you are in life, remember where you've come from, and take time to say thank you for never leaving me alone.

When in doubt read Margaret Rose powers," Footprints in the Sand." Because sometimes God needs to remind us of what he said," I will never leave you nor forsake you." To that my friend, you can say thank you and live a thanks full life.

Until next time, be encouraged.

The Chair

MY FRIEND AND I BOUGHT a very nice chair from a thrift store some time ago, it was black with white leather stitching and it looked brand-new. We saw other people looking at the chair, so we immediately purchased it and took it home. We proudly set it in the computer room, but to our amazement when we sat in the chair it did not perform properly. We were so disappointed that we had this beautiful chair, but it did not work correctly.

It was a swivel chair that was supposed to lean backward, but instead of leaning backward it would only lean forward. We were very disappointed, but at least we had a very nice chair sitting in the computer room. Now we have two chairs sitting in the computer room, both are swivel chairs and one works properly, and one doesn't. It became so irritating to sit in the chair, although it's very comfortable and looks good; it only leans forward and when you attempt to get up out of it the chair leans forward and you slide downward.

I tried to turn the knob in the back of it, I tried to adjust it by the handle on the side of it but nothing worked. So, I gave up on the chair, and I said to myself now I know why the previous owner gave it away. The chair sat in the computer room for two weeks, I really hated sitting in it because it didn't work correctly. One day a friend came over to work on my computer, and he said that's a nice chair; I said yes, it is but it doesn't work properly.

He said what you mean it doesn't work properly? I explained to him the problems I was having with the chair. He examined the chair and said whoever assembled the chair assembled it backward. That's why it's not working properly. I said you have got to be kidding me, is that why it's not functioning properly? The chair sat in the computer room for another two weeks, I got out of bed one night at 2 o'clock in the morning because I couldn't sleep, and I went and sat at the kitchen table and I began to pray.

I remember feeling very frustrated, because it seemed to me that I was not accomplishing my goals, my dreams or my vision that I believed God had given me for my life. I began to read the Book of Psalms, and it said, "God inhabits the praises of his people." So, I just began to praise God out loud, walking through my house just praising God out loud. As I walked in and out of every room praising God, I was led into my computer room and I begin to tell God that I need to turn my life around.

Then God brought to my spirit the chair that I had purchased, and how it needed to be turned around before it could function the way that it was meant to function. I was still praying and praising God as I rolled the chair into the kitchen so that I could look at it closer, because just as the chair needed to be turned around to function properly, so did I. As I turned the chair upside down to work on it, I saw the instructions on the bottom of it.

The previous owners did not read the instructions, because it clearly stated how the hardware was to be positioned on the bottom of the chair for it to work properly. Then I realized that I had not been following God's instructions that are clearly stated in my Bible for my life to function properly. Then I began to see clearly why our lives are in such shambles and chaos, because we have not followed clearly stated instructions.

The instructions are there, but we choose to ignore them, because we feel that we can do it ourselves. I remember assembling a bicycle, but I had some spare parts left over. Had I read the instructions there would not have been extra parts left over, who needs instructions right? I was in the same situation as the chair that needed repair. Our young people are in the same situation, in need of repair, the families are in the same situation, in need of repair. We need to turn our lives around, because we are not functioning properly; we are not performing at our maximum potential.

I then went to get my tools to turn the hardware around on the bottom of the chair. Then I saw that I needed a special kind of tool to take the hardware off and turn it around the proper way in order that the chair could function properly. Again, I knew that I needed something out of the ordinary to turn my life around, and so does our youth, our families, and society. Fortunately, I had access to the right tools to make the proper adjustments and now the chair functions properly.

We also have access to the only one that can change our lives, our youth and our families. But we must be willing to follow his instructions, seek first the kingdom of God, and his righteousness and all these things shall be added unto you. Are you ready to turn your children, and loved one's life around? Are you ready to turn your life around? Be encouraged friends and read the instructions.

The Choice

WHEN I WAS A CHILD I believed everything someone said about me, because I didn't know any better. Throughout my entire life I struggled with my identity, I always questioned my thoughts, my actions, and of course my decisions. I remember being told as a child in Mississippi that a black man could not succeed in this world, and I believed that. At that time, I thought it was a true statement, but later in life I learned that it was only true in my mind.

Not everyone has the same situations, circumstances or opportunities available to them in their lives. What I did learn was that a black man could not succeed in that world at that time, but now African-American people have the chance to make the choices to better themselves, their family, their community and society. It's not the chance that brings success, but it is the choice that makes success even possible. I feel that we as African-Americans have come such a long way, and endured so much hardship, but we have forgotten what the struggle was about.

The struggle was about taking the shackles off our hands and feet, being free to live where we wanted to, to be educated and have good jobs, to raise our families and teach our children that they can make a difference in this world. We as a people cannot afford to have the shackles taken off our hands and feet, only to have them placed on the hearts and minds of our future generation. No longer are we being beaten and killed by another race of people, but now our own children are doing it to themselves.

Our angry young African-American males are having shoot outs in the street, as though they are in the wild, wild, west. They engage in drive-by shootings with no regard for their lives or the lives of others. Drugs, gangs, and violence have taken over the city, yet we complain about the police shooting our young men and throwing them into jails and prisons.

It looks as though it's okay for African-Americans to kill other African-Americans, but if the police shoot and kills an African-American that's when we become outraged. Please don't misunderstand me, we should be outraged and march against injustice and protest wrongdoing, but we should also hold ourselves accountable for teaching our children to do what's right and to respect authority and make the right choices for themselves.

We should be outraged at our young people killing each other, and having no regard for authority or our elders, and how drugs are destroying our communities and families. We should be outraged about our young African-American men who have fathered children that they can't afford to take care of, and that they have no education or job skills or jobs to pay child support.

We should be outraged at our young women and girls, as they lay down and have these precious children that grandparents and the government must take care of. We should be outrage that the drug dealers have taken over our streets, we should be outraged at the fatherless generation that is coming up around us, and we should be outraged at the low turnout at the polls to vote.

Yet we complain about injustice and inequality. As I said earlier, we may not have the tools, techniques, and abilities to change the world, but we can always make the choice that creates the chance to change our lives. We have the same opportunities as everyone else, no one said it was going to be easy but it's possible. Turning your life around is never easy, going against tradition, having your friends talk about you, having a larger vision for yourself and your life is never easy.

This is the choice that one must make if they are to succeed. Putting down a gun and picking up a book, pulling up your pants and putting down a bad attitude. We must stop saying it's impossible and start saying I'm possible. We must remember that we can do all things through Christ who strengthen us. It's ok., you will probably fail a time or two, but you must hold on to your dreams. Les Brown, one of the greatest motivational speakers in the world said," if you fall try to land on your back, because if you can look up, you can get up." We will always have a choice, you must learn to make the right choice to change your life. Be encouraged my friends, when you choose Christ, he gives you power to do all things.

The Enemy is After our Children

WHAT'S GOING ON? IS SOMETHING in the water or the food that we eat? Is there a continual full moon? I say that we are in a spiritual fight for our children, our families, our homes, our neighborhoods, and our very lives. This is exactly what spiritual war feels like. We can't see the battle being waged, but we see the casualties in our homes, our families, our schools, and on the streets of our cities. I am reminded what John 10:10 (NKJV) says, the thief comes to steal, to kill, and to destroy."

I work at a school and I see students in the office first thing in the morning, and some of them are there daily. I asked them why are they in the office? It's always the same answer, it was someone else's fault, and some of them never take responsibility for their own actions and choices. The thief comes to steal; you may ask me how is the thief stealing from our children?

I'm so glad you asked me that question. When the students are sent out of the room for a timeout, a timeout from what? From what they came to school to do. From what their parents sent them to school to obtain. They came to school to get an education, not to sit in the office and play games while their classmates get gets an education. The enemy is stealing precious time that the students can never retrieve.

Every time a student is removed from the classroom, more valuable time is being stolen by the enemy. When the parents and guardians are called to come to school, some only think that their child is being picked on by the teacher. They cannot see the source of the battle, or how the enemy is stealing their children's precious time and education. The enemy comes to Kill, what is the enemy killing and how is he doing it?

The enemy is killing the children's hopes and dreams; he is filling their mind with negative self-talk, fear, doubt, and low self-esteem. He is killing their spirit with subtle messages that comes through TV, the Internet, social media, peer pressure, and even some of the very same people in their own home. It's like the enemy is extracting the values, morals, respect and empathy out of the children. I am reminded of a fishing trip that I went on up north near Long Lake Wisconsin, we went to a place called Lost Lake.

When we arrived, it was a very peaceful looking Lake with great looking fishing spots all around the lake. As I was making my way through the trail, I came upon the largest spider-web that I had ever seen in my life. It stretched across dozens of bushes, and I could see that it was full of pan fish bugs. These bugs that are called hellgrammites were brown and transparent, and all that was left was the empty shell that remained of this normally green bug.

God brought my mind to how a spider feeds on its prey, it captures the prey in its web and injects it with venom that liquefies the inside and then the spider drinks its dinner. In the same manner the enemy is draining the children of their moral compass, reasons, values, and common sense. The enemy comes to destroy, and finally, the children are destroying each other, because their parents have left them to themselves.

How can you build on nothing, you must first lay a firm foundation to build on? Family, faith, hope, love, integrity, these pillars of life are being destroyed because this is what the enemy came to tear down. Where are the parents while this atrocity is occurring? Some of them are missing in action. It's not too late to redeem our children back from the enemy's grip, but we must remember what the last part of John 10:10 (NKJV) says" Jesus said", I have come that you might have life and that you might have it more abundantly. Let us choose to give life back to our children. It's not too late. Be encouraged my friends.

The Garage Door

WHEN I LEAST EXPECTED IT, when I thought that I would go home put my feet up, kick back and relax; that's when it happened. After a long week of work and working that Saturday morning for Breakfast and Hoops at Frank school and doing my radio show, I thought I was going home and relax for the rest of the day. Earlier that Saturday morning when I left my home to go to work my garage door was working properly.

But as I arrived back home at 1: 30pm I pressed the remote control to open the garage door, it opened with no problem. After I parked inside and grabbed my briefcase out of the backseat and walked out of the garage door, I pressed the button to close the door. As I press the button the door went down, but it came off the track at the top of the garage and left a large opening between the garage door and the top of the garage. My hopes for a relaxing afternoon went out of the window or should I say out through the top of the garage door.

The only thing that I could think about was how much would it cost to repair the door. As I let the garage door back up to its open position, I saw a bracket on the ground beside where the door came to rest on the garage floor. I picked up the bracket from the door and began to examine where it might fit on the door by comparing it to the other side of the garage door. I located where the bracket was supposed to fit on the door, but I could not find the wheel that fitted inside the track that held the garage door in place.

I knew the wheel had to be in the garage on the floor somewhere, because the only place it could fall was down on the garage floor. I began by sweeping the garage floor, then moving my motorcycle, my ATV and my barbecue grill; but I could not find that wheel anywhere. I even let the door down partially to try and track where the wheel could have fallen, but that was to no avail. I knew that the wheel could have only fallen on one side of the garage, but in my desperation to find the wheel I searched the entire garage thinking it could have rolled under something.

After an hour of unproductively tearing my garage apart, I finally came to my senses and ask for help because I knew I could not complete this task by myself. Some of our young people are doing the same thing with their lives, they are trying to fix what's wrong, but they can't find the right pieces and they don't know how to ask for help. Maybe this is your situation also, you know something is broken and you just can't find the missing piece that will put your life back on track, but you don't know how to ask for help.

Look around you at the broken homes, the broken families, the broken dreams, and most importantly the broken people. Brokenness is all around us, but if you will ask people how they are doing they will say I am doing fine. One of my favorite passage says," Ask, and it shall be given to you, seek and you shall find, knock and the door shall be opened to you." For a very long time I had a big problem with asking people for help, because I was always the one to lend a helping hand and I didn't know how to ask for the help that I needed.

It doesn't matter how big and strong you are, or how financially stable you are, you will need help at some junction in your life. My garage door proved to me that I needed help not only in finding the wheel, but also in repairing the door and placing it back on track. I called a friend to help me find the wheel and we prayed before we started, and after thorough examination of the garage floor we concluded that it was not on the floor.

Then my friend asked me, "did I look on top of the garage door? And of course, I argued that it had to have fallen on the floor. So, he said let the garage door down, and I said why? The wheel had to fall on the floor somewhere. So, I gave in and let the garage door down. Just over half way down the wheel tumbled from atop the garage door. He looked directly at me and I hung my head in shame and apologized. We put on our gloves and together we repaired the garage door and put the wheel back in its track, and the door worked fine.

Oh yes, after that life lesson I did manage to grab a bite to eat, kick my feet up and relax. Friends, if something in your life is broken, don't be afraid to ask for help and don't be afraid to pray because prayer changes things. Ask, and you shall receive, seek and you shall find, knock and the door shall be opened unto you. Be encouraged.

Encouraged to have a heart transplant

IN THE BOOK OF EZEKIEL Chapter 36:27 (NKJV) says," I will give you a new heart and put a new spirit within you; I will take the heart of stone out of your flesh and give you a heart of flesh." I heard a story some time ago about a black crow and a white dove who were best friends, they went everyplace together, and they did everything together; mostly bad things.

They were associated and recognized not because of their different color, but because of the same evil intent and thoughts in their heart. After the death of the black crow and although the dove was as white as snow, all everyone else recognized about him was the black evil heart inside of him. The moral of the story, you may not be known by the color of your skin, but you will be known by the contents of your heart. Lately I have found myself with a harden heart toward certain people, and I know that's wrong of me, but some people just tend to rub you the wrong way.

I cannot be held responsible for the way that someone else acts toward me, but I am responsible for the way that I act toward another person. Because I oversee the words that come out of my mouth, and I oversee the actions that I take toward another person. So therefore,

I must guard my heart and my mouth. As I look at the political arena I see that it reflects the attitude of most of the world, and if this is the attitude of our would-be leaders then maybe those that follow them are of the same persuasion.

Everyone has a difference of opinion on every subject, but just because we do not agree on a matter does not mean that we must annihilate the opposing human being. Our words have power in them, therefore we must be very careful of what we say to other people and to ourselves. Our words are like a hammer that drives a nail into the wall, you can remove the nail from the wall, but the hole remains. We say hurtful words and then say we're sorry, we take back what was said but the pain of our words is still there.

Luke 6:45 (NKJV) says," a good man out of the good treasure of his heart brings forth good; and an evil man out of the evil treasure of his heart brings forth evil. For out of the abundance of the heart his mouth speaks. I found it so necessary and comforting when I read Ezekiel 27:36 (NKJV) that said," I will give you a new heart and put a new spirit within you; I will take the heart of stone out of your flesh and give you a heart of flesh."

I even see the heart of stone in some of our children, a rebellious and angry spirit that leads them further into darkness and ambiguity. The question was asked of Fat Joe the rapper, "why are our children so angry? "His response was," everyone wants to be hard." I heard someone say," whatever is in the well, will come up in the bucket. In relationship to your heart, whatever is in the deep part of your heart will come to the surface when you speak and act.

An evil man out of the evil treasure of his heart brings forth evil, when you get angry does the evil man show up and bring evil treasure out of his heart or does the good man show up and bring good treasures out of his heart? Whatever man shows up first (good or evil) dictates the outcome of the matter, can you afford to say the wrong words at the wrong time? I don't know about you, but I must guard my heart always, because sometimes evil thoughts will try to creep in and take root.

Remember, out of the abundance of the heart the mouth speaks; so, you must be careful about what takes root in your heart. If you have developed a root of bitterness in your heart toward someone or a certain people, it can be removed with a heart transplant. 2nd Corinthians 5:17 (NKJV) says," therefore, if anyone is in Christ, he is a new creation; old things have passed away; behold, all things have become new." Is there someone that you can share that scripture with, or is it you that need to hear it? It doesn't matter what you were in the past.

You could have been a failure, a loser, a drunkard, sexual immoral, or addicted to any number of things. However, once you receive Jesus Christ into your life, you get a chance to start all over again. You are a brand-new person and a brand-new creation in Jesus Christ. You now find your identity in Christ and in his word. You are a brand-new person, fully equipped to live a victorious life. You may ask yourself, is it really that easy? Yes, it is.

The wonderful thing about this heart transplant that I'm referring to, there is no waiting lists, there is no astronomical fee, you don't have to go through a painful surgery, no recovery room to wait in, you don't even have to leave your home. My friends, you can receive a heart transplant right now, right here this very minute, and it's free because the price has been prepaid already for you; and all you must do is ask for.

Believe it and receive it, because all things are possible to them that believe. Be encouraged today my friends because God loves you. Remember what he said," I will give you a new heart and put a new spirit within you I will take the heart of stone out of your flesh and give you a heart of flesh. Here is the million-dollar question, are you ready for a character transformation? Be encouraged my friends.

The Humpty Dumpty syndrome

WE HAVE ALL HEARD THE nursery rhyme about Humpty Dumpty. It goes like this," Humpty Dumpty sat on the wall, Humpty Dumpty had a great fall, all the king's horses and all the king's men, could not put Humpty Dumpty together again." This is my version." Humpty Dumpty sat on the wall, Humpty Dumpty had a great fall, all the king's horses, all the king's men, and all the king's programs could not put Humpty Dumped together again." How many Humpty Dumpty do you know that are still broken in their 30s 40s 50s and 60s? There are thousands of broken people everywhere, but if you look into their eyes you would not see a trace of brokenness.

Their life however, tells a different story. The king's programs utilize the Jail and prison system as a revolving door for some of these Humpty Dumpty's. The king's men call the revolving door recidivism, recidivism is the act of a person repeating or relapsing into an undesirable behavior after they have experienced negative consequences, or punishment, for that behavior. They may have been treated or trained to extinguish that behavior but have still reverted. Because they are still broken, all the king's horses, all the king's men, and all the king's programs cannot put Humpty Dumpty together again.

I don't know about you, but I was one of the thousands of broken Humpty Dumpty's in the world. I tried changing my mind about various assumptions and traditions, I tried changing my bad habits and turning them into positive and productive ones. I even tried running away to a new city, but it was not a new city that I needed, it was a new heart. My old way of thinking only offered a temporal solution to my brokenness. Whatever caused Humpty Dumpty to fall off the wall is beyond me, but I know that all the king's horses, all the king's men, and all the king's programs could not put me together again.

The king's programs only repaired my external, but it took Jesus Christ to repair my internals by giving me a new heart. King David, one of the most famous kings in the Bible asked God in Psalm 51:10 (NKJV)," Create in me a clean heart oh God, and renew within me a right spirit. King David had sinned by committing adultery and murder. He did not call upon an earthly king, he knew that he needed a clean heart. So, he called upon the King of Kings because he knew his sins had pushed him off the wall.

What has pushed you off the wall? Maybe your brokenness came through a medical condition. Or maybe from stress, depression, anxiety, mental illness, or some other problems. Maybe alcohol and other drugs caused you to fall off the wall. Maybe you committed murder or adultery, and you cannot forgive yourself. Maybe you are wrestling with guilt, doubt, and shame. Whatever the problems are, all the king's horses, all the king's men cannot put you back together again. Broken homes, broken lives, broken families, broken dreams, and broken people are all around us and are desperate for the truth. Our young people are being led away from the truth at an alarming rate, and they too are suffering from the Humpty Dumpty syndrome. They are being pushed off the wall by external and internal pressures and situations, that has but one cure.

Stressful life events and low levels of communication with parents may also be significant risk factors. Our young people are about twice as likely to attempt suicide, but our young men are at a much greater risk.

Many of our youth are sitting on the wall with the wrong role models, and they are listen to all the negative self-talk that is being said. Many of our youth will have a great fall, because they have not been told the truth. John 8:32 (NKJV) says," And you shall know the truth, and the truth shall make you free." The king's programs are failing to address the real issues that are going on in our teenager's lives as well as in our own lives, we all need a new heart now more than ever. The book of Ezekiel says," A new heart will I give you, and a new spirit will not put within you: and I will take away the stony heart out of your flesh, and I will give you a heart of flesh".

It's time to stop generational brokenness, it stops with you and me, our young people don't need another motto to say, they need a model to see. We know the way and we must show the next generation the way, so that they can lead by example. Be encouraged my friends, the truth will break down the walls.

The joy of serving others

I WAS INVITED TO A retirement party for a friend and a coworker recently, who had faithfully given years of service to a great organization. We all gathered at a small place out in Lake Geneva called Lake Geneva school of cooking. The school was nestled in an old Baptist Church that had been turned into a store and a restaurant. From the outside one would not know that such a place existed inside this historical building.

I was told that my boss orchestrated the whole shebang over a year ago, never would we have imagined the treat that was in store for us inside a cooking school. It was truly one of Lake Geneva's best kept secrets, hidden right in the middle of downtown. So, when we all arrived, my boss was waiting on the porch for us, and took us through the store to the dining room area which was beautifully decorated.

As we made our way through the hallway to the kitchen and pass a huge wine rack, in the huge opening of the kitchen stood a very long counter with all types of ingredients and goodies on it. Suddenly he appeared, Chef John the Master Chef. With a Boston accent, signature chef hat, apron and shirt with black short pants, and a black mustache. Armed to the teeth with wit and humor, one of the friendliest guys I've ever met.

He. Introduced himself and his staff, and he told us about his accomplishments and how long he had been in the restaurant business, just a wealth of information. After we introduced ourselves to him and his staff, he personally remembered all our names and poured us a glass of sparkling wine or Perrier water. As he began to tell us what the evening would entail, the fragrance of the appetizers that were in the oven began to fill the air.

By this time every one of us was drooling at the mouth and waiting to be unleashed upon the appetizers that was now staring us in the face and ready for consumption. Chef John had such a joy about himself while serving others, I saw the same joy in my boss and in my coworker that was retiring. The evening had been planned out so perfectly and thoughtfully, I don't know if it was the wine that made everything go so well or if it was the friendship, camaraderie, and working together as a team, or the joy and love that goes into serving one another.

I'm pretty sure it was the components that were shared in the serving of others, the food and the wine just made it that much better. Then Chef John laid out the menu for the night. Shrimp Briana kaiulani, macadamia nut pesto, angel hair pasta. Baby greens with pecans and smoked bacon, shaved goat cheese, and honey Dijon dressing. Chicken medallions with prosciutto, sherry wine reduction. Kahlua espresso brownie.

Everything came with the ingredients, directions, and plating, the cloves garlic, the extra virgin olive oil, lemon juice, basil leaves, everything that we needed to make the dinner and to serve each other was there. Did I mention the wine, sparkling wine that is. We were divided into teams; each team had a dish to prepare and they were responsible for the preparation of that dish. Chef John gave instructions, encouragement, and more wine to every team.

I have not had that much fun in the kitchen in a long time, the music began to play, bodies began to sway, and we were shaking our groove thing all over the place. What fun we all had, cooking, laughing, dancing, serving each other and loving it. We all took part in the preparation, cooking, plating, and serving. As we move to the dining room to enjoy our creations, Chef John reminded us all how we all had participated in this great meal and how it had all come together through service and teamwork.

Each team brought in their own creation that they had prepared and informed the other teams of how they had prepared their creations. Every team applauded their teammates, and the effort that was put forward to serve in this retirement party for our dear friend. My favorite book has a lot to say about service, Matthew 25:35 – 45(NKJV).

It talks about the separation of the sheep and the goats, for I was hungry and you gave me food; I was thirsty and you gave me something to drink; I was a stranger and you took me in; I was naked and you clothe me; I was sick and you visited me; I was in prison and you came to me. Then the righteous will answer him, saying Lord, where did we see you hungry and feed you, or thirsty and gave you something to drink? When did we see you a stranger and took you in, or naked and clothe you?

When did we see you sick, or in prison, and come to you? And the king will answer and say to them, assuredly, I say to you, since you did it for one of the least of these my brother, you did it to me. Then he will also say to those on the left hand, depart from me you curse, into the everlasting fire prepared for the devil and his angels: for I was hungry and you gave me no food; I was thirsty and you gave me nothing to drink; I was a stranger and you did not take me in, naked and you did not clothe me, sick and in prison and you did not visit me, then they will answer him, saying Lord, when did we see you hungry or thirsty or a stranger or naked or sick or in prison, and did not minister to you?

Then he will answer them say, assuredly, I say to you and is much as you did not do it to one of the least of these, you did not do it to me. We all have been called to serve in some capacity, when we serve, others are blessed, and we can make a difference in their lives. We can't all build houses, or run for president, but we all can serve and help others. Jesus came to serve, and not to be served. Should we not do the same, because there is joy in serving.

The life lesson series

LIFE DOES NOT ALWAYS GO according to plans, situations occur that requires us to examine our lives and pinpoint the problems and seek out solutions. My last article the chair, was one of those situations that caused me to take a closer look at my life through a series of events. The chair was the perfect example for me to see how backward my life was, and how it needed to be turned around to function properly.

I believe circumstances occur in our lives that mimic our situations, and if we are real with ourselves and open to change, we can find solutions to our own problems as we observe and examine the situations that are presented before us. I was motivated to write about the chair, because I found inspiration for my life as I began to turn the mechanisms on the bottom of the chair in the right direction that would cause it to work properly and serve its purpose.

I believe that life lessons offer us an opportunity to observe, examine, and apply what we learn from everyday occurrence that we might be more productive in own our lives. Just last Saturday after Christmas, I was hit with another life lesson that happened with my garage door. That lesson had many applications that I can apply to various areas in my life. I will tell you more about that observation next year in my series.

I have been so inspired by life lessons that I will begin writing a series on life lessons. My prayers and hopes are that you will be encouraged and inspired to examine your own life to find what you need to do to be the best you ever and achieve your full potential. Be encouraged my friends.

The lost car keys

IN HIS BOOK, "MAXIMIZING YOUR potential," Dr. Myles Munroe says, "God's intent for men and women has not changed, nor has he taken from us the strength and beauty he gave us at birth. These gifts are buried within us, covered over by the attitudes and assumptions that prevent us from living the abundant life God planned for us. In effect, many have placed a no trespassing sign over the power, strength, ability, talent, and capabilities that God has given each of us."

Because we have obeyed that sign, many of the possibilities with which we were born still exist within us hidden dormant, unused and untried." It is up to us to recognize and remove the barriers that hinder and hide our potential. We absolutely must move the small things out of our way to get to what is necessary to make our lives a success. Three weeks ago, on a Monday morning I was preparing to go to work, my Monday morning meeting with staff was scheduled for 9 o'clock.

Armed with everything I needed for the day, I headed for the door. Where are my car keys I asked myself? I have a meeting in half an hour and I can't afford to be late. My car keys were not in the usual place, so I backtracked my every step. I turned the house upside down looking for the keys and I traced my steps over and over. I checked my coat pockets and my pant pockets. I even went outside to look in the driveway. I opened the garage and looked in the garage on the floor, and under my truck.

I went back in the house and started all over again to look for the keys, starting in the kitchen and back through the living room again, I looked in the couch and under the couch. I looked in the exercise room, in the closet and in my jacket pockets. I looked in the computer room, in my desk and under my desk. I looked on the bed and under the bed also, I looked in the bathroom on the floor and under the rugs. I still can't find my keys anywhere, now I go back to the garage and look through my windows on my truck to look if I can see the keys in the truck.

At this point I can't even think straight, trying to remember where I placed the spare key on my truck. But I can't remember that either. I'm all dressed to go to work, but now I must get on my knees and feel under the back of the truck to find my extra key that I hid from myself. I cannot find the extra key, even after laying on my back on the garage floor in a small puddle of water. I got up off the floor of the garage and went back in the house and called my staff and informed them that I would have to cancel our morning meeting.

One of my staff people ask if anything was wrong, I felt so embarrassed to tell her that I have lost my keys and I am locked out of my truck. I am standing in the kitchen by the sink and counter still looking for those elusive car keys. I remember moving everything on the countertop except for that bag of corn chips, I know I looked all around the bag of chips, I did not see those keys.

Something within my spirit said to move the bag of chips, but I resisted and said there's no way that the keys can be there; because I have already looked around the bag. After an hour of looking for those keys, laying down in a small puddle of water on the garage floor. Canceling my staff meeting and being totally embarrassed, I'm sure you can guess what was under the bag of corn chips, those elusive car keys which was staring me straight in the face.

All I really had to do, to save myself all the trouble I had gone through was to move a small bag of corn chips, I could have avoided all the headaches and disappointments of the last hour. How much greater could life be if we were to move some of the small things from of our lives? Countless headaches, heartaches, and disappointments could be avoided. Maybe we could accomplish our goals earlier in life, with greater success. An attitude is a small thing that makes a tremendous difference in our lives.

A bad attitude is like a flat tire, if you don't change it, you'll never go anywhere. Attitude is everything. Attitude can make you or break you. Unfortunately, some of our lives are broken and destroyed because of a small thing called "attitude". The Bible says," we are to remove the plank from our own eye, and then we will see clearly to remove the speck from our brother's eye. Maybe it's time to move the small things out of our lives, so that we can help others move the mountains out of their lives and move on to greater success. Be encouraged my friends.

The Potter and the Clay

WE SOMETIMES QUESTION WHY GOD allows us to go through some of the trials and tribulations we go through. I believe this little teacup story will answer a lot of questions for us. God knows what is needed and what he is doing, whether we understand it or not. The story of the little teacup reveals much. There was a couple who took a trip to England to shop in a beautiful antique store to celebrate their 25th wedding anniversary. They both loved antiques and pottery, and especially teacups.

Spotting an exceptional cup, they asked" may we see that cup?" We've never seen such a beautiful cup." As the lady handed it to them, suddenly the teacups spoke and said," you don't understand." I have not always been this beautiful teacup." There was a time when I was just a lump of red clay." Then the little tea cup begin to tell the story of what it used to be, before The Master remade it. I am reminded of what my mother used to say, she would say," I might not be what I ought to be but thank God I am not what I use to be." What she was saying," was that she was like that little teacup when it was a lump of clay before God (The Master) reshaped it." I have said that same phase that my mother said repeatedly in my life." I might not be what I ought to be but thank God I am not what I use to be." Just like the little teacup in the story, I think back to what I was before The

Master remade me. Before He reshaped me, I had nothing of beauty or worth to give to those around me. Because my mind, heart, and spirit were so distorted that nothing of worth could have come from my life. But when The Master placed me on His potter's wheel, it was a life changing experience. In Jeremiah 18:2 – 7(NKJV), God spoke to Jeremiah and said," Arise and go down to the potter's house, and there I will cause you to hear my words." Then I went down to the potter's house, and there he was, making something at the wheel.

And the vessel that he made of clay was marred in the hand of the potter; so, he made it again into another vessel, as it seemed good to the potter to make. Then the words of the Lord came to me, saying: "O house of Israel, can I not do with you as this potter?" says the Lord. "Look, as the clay is in the potter's hand, so are you in My hand, O house of Israel! The moral of the story is this: God knows what He's doing for each of us. He is the Potter, and we are His clay. He will mold us and make us and expose us to just enough pressures of just the right kind that we may be made into a flawless piece of work to fulfill his good, pleasing and perfect will.

Have you ever felt like that lump of clay? Has the world beat the life out of you? Has it stolen your identity, made you to feel useless, and thrown you away? No matter who you are, or what you have gone through you are not useless. God can take what the world sees as nothing and turn it into something beautiful. Sometimes we are distorted and disfigured, by the views and opinions of others, worldviews, family traditions, and even our own thinking. Just like the Potter who reshaped the clay that had been marred, God can reshape and remold us into something that brings beauty into the world. Be encouraged my friends, God is not finished with you yet.

The power of faith

THERE IS A STORY IN the Bible about a woman who was suffering and bleeding for 12 years, she went to various doctors and they could not heal her, and she exhausted all her earnings. In the book of Luke 8:43 – 48 (NKJV), and it reads," now a woman, having a flow of blood for 12 years who had spent all her livelihood on physicians and could not be healed by any, came from behind and touched the border of Jesus garment. And immediately her flow of blood stopped. Jesus said, "who touched me? When all denied it, Peter and those with him said, "Master, the multitudes throng and press you, and you say, who touched me?

But Jesus said, somebody touched me, for I perceive power going out from me." Now when the woman saw that she was not hidden, she came trembling; and falling before him, she declared to him in the presence of all the people the reason she had touched him and how she was healed immediately. And he said to her, "daughter, be of good cheer," your faith has made you well. Go in peace. The woman described in this passage had enough faith to reach out and touch the hem of Jesus garment. When she did, Jesus felt power leaving his body and healing the woman. He told her, "your faith has made you well."

Many people in our time also are looking for healing, and Jesus Christ has the genuine power to provide that healing and to save lives. The power of faith when believed and acted upon can move mountains and take you to places you would not normally go. Let me paint a picture for you, imagine if you will a woman bent over in pain, going from doctor to doctor trying to find a cure for her issue of blood. She gave everything she had to be made whole, but no one could help her. Then one day she heard that Jesus was coming to town, she had no money left, but she had faith and she said," if I can just touch the hem of his garment I will be made whole."

I can imagine this little lady in pain, pushing her way through the crowd of people and allowing no one to stand in her way. There were so many people that day that had their own special needs that wanted Jesus to touch them, but this little lady was desperate, and she said," if I can just touch the hem of his garment. She knew where the power was, for the power was in Jesus and he had the power to do what no other person could do. When she touched his garment, he felt the power go out of him and he knew that someone had great faith. And he asked his disciples," who touched me?

Verse 47 says, now when the woman saw that she was not hidden, she came trembling; and falling down before him, she declared to him in the presence of all the people the reason she had touched him. I can imagine this little lady saying," Lord I heard of your healing power, and I believe you are who you say you are and I needed a miracle. I've gone to every doctor in the land and no one could help me, but when I heard that you were coming I knew that there was hope." How many of us are just like that little lady? We have our own individual issues that we have struggled with for years and have gotten no better.

As a matter of fact, we pass these issues on to our children and they struggle with the same issues that has plagued us. When do we stop the bleeding that is destroying our lives and our children lives?

This little woman reached out and touch the hem of Jesus' garment. When she did this, the actual power of God went out from Jesus' body and healed her. Jesus could feel the power of God leaving his body to heal her. It was like a divine surge of energy flowing from him into her. Christians who have received this same power can minister anywhere and anytime in the same manner that Jesus did.

When they have been filled with God's power, they can release this power into the lives of their children and loved ones to heal them, to set them free, and to speak blessings into their lives. When the gospel of Jesus Christ is communicated to others, it is only effective to the degree that this power is being transmitted. Our faith must be strong, and we must have no doubt in our heart that Jesus is able to heal any issues that come our way. Even the power of Jesus can be blocked because of unbelief that we carry in our heart. Unbelief short-circuits God's power and blocks the flow of the miraculous.

It doesn't matter if this unbelief is due to a hardness of heart, cynicism, or even theology. The result is that God's power is kept from operating. God does not ask his people to be mindless or gullible. However, he does ask that we believe what he says he can do in his word. With all the fear, doubt, and hardness of heart that is prevalent in the world today, we must increase our faith that we might be able to help our sisters and brothers that are dealing with serious life issues.

I talked with a lady the other day that was going through primarily the same thing in which this little lady went through. She told me that she was sick and that she was going back and forth to see various doctors, but the doctors could not find the cause of her problems. As we talked I could see the pain that she was in on her face, but all the doctors told her was that the pain was in her head because they could not find any evidence in her body. After we finished talking

I prayed for her and asked her to go back to the doctor because she truly was in pain. The issues that she was having, her son was having the same issues.

Therefore, this article is so important, because we have children that are going through the very same issues that we struggle with and we need to tell them that Jesus can heal all their illnesses. Jesus said," all things are possible to him that believe. Not doubting but having faith the size of a mustard seed. Instead of telling God how big your problem is, let's show our problems how big our God is. My friend, you have healing power through faith in Jesus Christ. Do you know someone who can use a miracle today? Use the power of faith to turn a life around, be encouraged.

The Power of Fear

FEAR OF FAILURE, FEAR OF man, fear of consequences, fear of moving forward, fear of being lonely, fear of dying, fear of using all your gifts, talents and abilities will keep you crammed in a corner. It's going to take courage and strength beyond your capacity to step out of the box that the world wants to keep you in, because the power of fear will paralyze you and you will remain confined to that box. Charles Spurgeon the great theologian said," the best and wisest thing in the world is to work as if it all depended upon you, and then trust in God, knowing that it all depends upon him."

In my own life fear, doubt and negative self – talk appears daily, and daily I must reinforce faith and positive thinking to remember who I am and whose I am. Life can be very scary at times, and it can appear that you are stuck between a rock and a hard place with no way out and nowhere to turn. Be honest with yourself, has life situations and circumstances ever made you so afraid that you regretted trying to change your life? Now you want to go back to where you were because it was easier to stay in a tough situation than to try and live in a new situation. Change can be overwhelming, and it can also bring a new beginning if fear is replaced with faith.

I'm reminded of the Red Sea crossing in the book of Exodus. There were literally hundreds of thousands of people following Moses out of the land of Egypt, men, women and children, young and old, healthy and sick people, some were being carried and some walking. They left with the dreams and hope of a better life, not knowing where they were going but anywhere was better than Egypt. Facing cruel taskmasters, being whipped and beaten, forced to make bricks without straw, barely enough food or water, any place was better than this place. Oh, the joy of being delivered from slavery, free at last, free at last, thank God almighty we are free at last.

The Red Sea was in the front of them, and on both sides, were hills, and mountains that were impossible for most of the people to pass. None of that mattered now, because they were free, and their dreams were just around the corner. But in the distant the dust from Pharaoh's horses and chariots could be seen. Pharaoh with his great army was coming down on the children of Israel, and the people became afraid as despair shattered their dreams, they panicked in unbelief and said to Moses," is this not the word that we told you in Egypt, saying, let us alone that we may serve the Egyptian?

For it would have been better for us to serve the Egyptians then that we should die in the wilderness. How many of us has allowed fear to shatter our dreams, destroy our hope and made us want to go back and live in the terrible situation that we came out of? The people would rather be slaves in chains and bondage, to be whipped and killed and sold from their families than to die in the wilderness as free men. Fear blinded their eyes and caused them to walk by sight, and not by faith.

They preferred their afflictions over faith and freedom, but little did they know that they were about to witness the miraculous. So, the Egyptians pursued them, all the horses and chariots of Pharaoh, and overtook them camping by the sea and Pi Hahiroth, before Baal Zephon. So, they were very afraid, and they cried out to Moses. And

Moses said to the people, do not be afraid. Stand still and see the salvation of the Lord which He will accomplish for you today.

When we replace fear with faith, our whole world changes because fear is dethroned, and faith is victorious. God told Moses to tell the people to go forward, fear can only stop you when you have no determination. God wants His people to go forward, not to the left nor the right but forward. We build up walls that God wants to tear down, fears that God must eradicate. Instead of us telling God how big our storms and fears are, we should tell our storms and fears how big our God is. Fear, doubt, and unbelief closed the people in, but one man's unshakable faith opened the Red Sea and the children of Israel walk through on dry land.

God has already made provision for our victory also, but fear will cause us to look down when we should be looking up. Fear causes us to take our eyes off God and look to ourselves, God knows how to run our lives better than we do. Jeremiah 29:11 (NKJV) says," for I know the thoughts that I think toward you, says the Lord, thoughts of peace and not of evil, to give you a future and a hope." God has assured your victory, do not allow fear to paralyze you in your tracks and stop you from moving forward. Fear has no power except that which we give it, God has not given us a spirit of fear, but of power, and of love, and a sound mind. Change your mind, change your life.

Too many Men hide from their responsibility.

ADAM, WHERE ARE YOU? GENESIS 3:9-10 (NKJV) says," and the Lord God called unto Adam and said unto him, where are you? And he said, "I heard your voice in the garden and I was afraid because I was naked; and I hid myself." God is still seeking you today and you are still hiding from God, but now is the time for you to come out of hiding and come back to your responsibilities and God. Adam, let's talk about some of the things that have happened in your absence. Your wife has been taken hostage by woman's libration, drugs and alcohol, perverse thinking and living, poverty, isolation, confusion and doubt.

Your wife, your mother and your daughters are living without natural covering, which should have been you. The women are turning to other women for physical, sexual, social and economic advantages. Adam, where are you? Since you have hidden from God, you have also hidden from your responsibilities, obligations and your duties to your family. Adam, it is your obligation to lead your family out of spiritual depravity.

It is your responsibility to be the spiritual covering for your family. Your family is being divided and destroyed, because you are not in your rightful place, you were hiding. When you get to where you are supposed to be, then God will be where he is supposed to be and that is at the head of your lives. Adam, where are you? Since you have been gone let me tell you what has happened to your home. Your home has been devastated and separated.

What was once a haven is now a cold empty place that harbors everything except hope, godly direction, holiness and of course you. Your home has been invaded by strangers that have no last names; like TV, CD, HD, DVD, PS2, N64, Xbox, I pad, and Android. These guys with no last names have brought things into your home that I know you would never allow (had you truly been there). This TV Guy is so cool. He takes your families mind off all their problems.

He has no problem talking to them about sex, drugs, or alcohol, things that you would never allow your family to be exposed to, (had you truly been there). The scary thing is that this TV guy is always there 24\7, 365 days a year. They say that TV is cool, but he has a powerful friend that will take them even places that TV doesn't even know about. They called him Internet. This guy can travel at the speed of light without getting a ticket and there isn't any place that he can't take them. He's very scary, you must watch this guy very closely.

Adam, where are you? Now let me tell you what has happened to your children. Adam, you better sit-down brother, we've got problems. John 10:10 (NKJV) says," the thief comes to steal, and to kill, and to destroy," Adam, when you were hiding from God, you were hiding from your responsibility to protect your family. When you left your family unprotected, you allow a thief to come in to steal, kill, and destroy your entire family.

The thief has stolen your boys. He has deceived them into thinking that they can be men in at an early age. By telling them that they can be fathers at the age of 14, telling them that drugs and alcohol will help them cope with the problems of life, telling them that they don't need an education. The thief has killed your boy's dreams through the desire to make fast money and disregard the law of the land. His chosen weapons are gangs, drugs, and violence. So many of your boys have died through making bad choices and getting caught up in the system. Adam, where are you?

Children making one poor choice after another, children having babies and they are still babies. Your children have no future, they have no respect for authority or most of their parents. Adam, do you really want to hear about your daughters? Your daughters have no idea how precious and special they truly are, so they live a life with uncertainty and doubt.

You weren't there to tell them how beautiful they look or how important they are, so the first boy that paid any attention to them and made them feel special they fell in love with. The first time out, pregnant, ashamed, afraid, abandoned, abortion, where are you? They are alone, they cry for daddy, but the only voices they hear is that of guilt, fear, and shame and the father of the child saying to get rid of it. Adam, are you still sitting? I didn't mention what is going on in the school.

Your children are not interested in getting an education, they would rather be a part of problems, than a part of the solution because they know that no one is at home to come and check on them or how they are behaving at school. The thief is doing a good job at stealing your family away from you and leading them down the wrong path. Now, here's the good news. The last part of that verse in John 10:10 (NKJV) says, but I have come that they might have life, and that they may have it more abundantly.

Your family needs abundant life today. If you will come out of hiding and be where you are supposed to be, then God will be where he is supposed to be. That is showing you how to be the effective leader that you were designed to be. You are the spiritual covering for your family. Adam, come back home and stand for something, because your family is falling for anything. They need you clothed and in your right mind, right now.

Treasure in the trash

I HEARD A STORY SOME time ago about two brothers that was raised by a single mother. One of the sons stayed in trouble all the time, dealing drugs, fighting, involved with gangs, in and out of jail, always into mischief. That old mother prayed diligently for that old no good son, that God would change him and turn his life around. The other son stayed home, went to school and got a great education. In fact, he became a doctor and his mother was so proud of him. He even met his future wife in college and they got married and had a couple of children.

He invited his mother to come and live with them to help take care of the children while he and his wife worked. The good son and his wife became very wealthy and lived in a mansion, by this time the mother had grown rather old and frail. The wife became unhappy with the old mother's language and she told her husband that the mother was using bad grammar in front of the children, and she refuse to have her children speaking that type of language. So, the wife suggested to her husband that they place his mother in a nursing home, her husband reluctantly agreed.

That night after dinner the good son told his mother that they were going to place her in a nursing home, the mother was very upset and began crying and said I'll do better, and I'll work harder. The son said," you're getting older now mother and you are using bad English around the children." We spent a lot of time looking for the right place for you, there's a lot of old people there, you will be around people your age, they have a big screen TV, and a swimming pool, you will love it there mother.

The next day the chauffeur pulled up in the long limousine and place the mother's luggage in the back; the good son and his mother got in and headed toward the nursing home. The mother's eyes were filled with tears as they pulled out of the driveway of the big mansion, the good son tried to comfort his mother, but she continued to cry. As they were going down the road an old car was coming toward them, it was that old no good son coming to see his mother. He looked into the limousine and saw her, he turned his car around and pulled up alongside of the limousine and motioned for the driver to pull over.

He got out of his old car and came up to the limousine and asked his brother," where are you taken my mother? The good son said," I'm taking her to the nursing home; mother is old now and we can't take care of her anymore. So, my wife and I decided that we would place her in a nursing home, where were you all this time? The old no good son said," I know I messed up so many times, but now I've cleaned my life up and I'm back to stay.

Mother, I know I haven't always done right by you, I broke your heart so many times, I made you cry countless tears; but I've changed. I don't drink, and I don't smoke, I don't run around anymore, I have a job now, I don't make much, I have a small apartment, with a small garden outside. I grow my own greens, beans, potatoes and tomatoes, I don't have much but mother you are welcome to come home with me.

You can sleep in the bed and I'll sleep on the couch, you don't have to go to a nursing home mother, come and go home with me, I love you mother and I'm sorry for all the pain that I caused you. Please forgive me mother, because I'm a changed man now. That old mother got out of that long limousine and got into that old beat up car with that old no good son. This was the one that everyone gave up hope on and through his name in the trash, but he turned out to be his mother's treasure.

He brought his mother to his home and he loved and cared of his mother until she went on to be with the Lord in glory. Do you have a child or a loved one that you have given up on and through their name in the trash and forgot about? From the day of his birth that old mother prayed continually for that old no good son, because she knew no matter how far he ran and how much trouble he got into God could still turn his life around. That old mother knew what the word of God said in 2 Corinthians 5:7 (NKJV), for we walk by faith, not by sight.

We cannot walk by faith if our eyes are focused on what we see going on around us. All that we see is subject to change; God's word will never change. This does not mean that our faith lies in denying the circumstances. God does not call those things that are as if they are not; instead he calls those things which do not exist as though they did. Walking by faith means aligning ourselves with God rather than with the circumstances; believe in God's testimony and living in agreement with it.

As people who walk by faith, not by sight, we are to live according to the truth of God's word and the testimony of his spirit. Are you walking by faith? Or are you walking by sight? If you have thrown a treasure in the trash, ask God to retrieve it and clean it up that it might bring beauty and value to someone's life. Please remember, you could be the treasure in the trash that the world has thrown away; but

I pray for you right now in the name of Jesus that you would realize how valuable you are and that you were made to bring beauty to someone's life. Walk by faith and not by sight. Until next time, be blessed my friends.

We need prayer warriors

WHERE ARE GOD'S PEOPLE? YOU know the ones who pray "Here am I Lord, send me, I will go". Where are the ones who will stand up for the word of God? Where are God's people that have a heart for the children and families that have been broken and left by the wayside? Please don't misunderstand my point. But there are so many social programs that are being supplemented for the word of God. What the world needs today is not more machinery, or better and new organizations, or more novel methods, but men and women of prayer that God can use to pour out his spirit upon.

I see government programs being cut daily, to take money from essential programs and legitimate needs only to spend them on nonessential items and wasteful ideas. Where is the church and God's people that will say, "Lord, may I be a blessing in this time of need? So many government programs are failing to meet the needs of the people, but larger jails and prisons are being built. Where is the church? Shouldn't we be building strong families? Or should we be promoting rock groups, festivals, and social programs?

There is a time and place for everything, but at a time like this we need God's people to be prayer warriors. In his book, The Battle for a Generation. Ron Hutchcraft talks about a stretch of the Atlantic coast called the graveyard of the Atlantic. Because of violent storms, shifting sands, and heavy shipping, the Outer Banks have witnessed hundreds of shipwrecks over the last three centuries. Therefore, the United States Life-Saving Service was so important in their days before the Coast Guard was born.

The Life Saving Service was, in fact, a spawning ground for heroes. It established its lifesaving stations every seven miles along the coast, big white frame buildings, built far enough back from the ocean to be protected from the storm's fury. The station was manned by an eight-man crew, and on one night a brutal storm had left four men stranded on a sinking vessel with only the mast above the water. The lifesaving crew members stood on the beach, contemplating the limited chances of their own boats surviving the three-mile trip to the site of the sinking ship.

The chances were good that they themselves might be swept out to sea. But they went anyway. Twenty - two hours without food or sleep, they work for eight battered hours against the storm, and they brought back all the men alive. In another storm, called the worst storm of the 19th century, a single lifesaving crewman plunge right into the violence surf to help people going down on a sinking ship offshore. He battled his way through the surf and the storm to bring back one survivor alive, then another, and another.

By the time he collapsed in exhaustion on the beach, he had single-handedly rescued all ten people aboard the sinking ship. Exploits like these put flesh on the courageous motto of the Life Saving Service, "You have to go out. You don't have to come back. We are in similar situations today, where the storms and surfs of life are destroying so many young people, children, and families. Just like those brave crewmembers, our rescue effort should begin when we hear the cries of dying people.

The heroes of the Life Saving Service knew their efforts were life or death, they plunge into the storm and the surf because they knew the people out there were dying. We all have heard the term, "Code Blue." In a medical environment, "Code Blue" is the summons to all personnel that this is a life or death emergency, one of which everyone drops what he or she is doing to respond. Social and governmental programs are being developed to put a Band-Aid on cancer. It looks good on the outside, but it does not help to heal the situation.

But the church has the answer, instead of a Band-Aid situation the church can go in where no government agency has gone before. Giving love and compassion that surpasses all understanding and lifting heavy burdens, not being judgmental of those involved, and not placing the blame on anyone or anything except sin. Society says that we can pass out condoms to protect our children from diseases, but we can't pass out Bibles to protect our children from sin and eternal damnation which is more devastating than any disease known to man.

It's not great talent, nor great learners, nor great preachers that God need, but man great in holiness, great in faith, great in love, great and integrity, and great in prayer. Prayer makes the man, prayer makes the preacher, prayer makes the pastor, prayer moves the church, and prayer changes the world and those in it. Throughout my teenage years my mother fervently prayed for me every day, I am who I am and what I am because I had a praying mother.

2nd Chronicles 7:14 (NKJV) says, "If my people, which are called by my name, shall humble themselves, and pray, and seek my face, and turn from their wicked ways; then will I hear from heaven, and will forgive their sins, and will heal their land. God promises to give us an answer. Psalms 91:15 (NKJV) says, "He shall call upon me, and I will answer him, I will be with him in trouble,

I will deliver him, and honor him." God is waiting on us to get to where we should be, and then he will do what he promised to do, it's your move people of God. Be encouraged and know that God answers prayers.

Where have all the father's gone

AT MY WORK, I RUN a program called", Boys Night Out". This program was originally intended for dads and boys to come and spend some time on a Friday night playing basketball, board games, air hockey, foosball, chess or checkers, eating pizza and just hanging out and having some fun at the gym. Over the years the boys did not stop coming, but dads stopped coming and the hungry boys increased. Not that they were hungry for food, but I believe they were hungry for that male role model that most of them did not have at home.

On an average Boys Night Out event, 30 to 50 boys will attend. One month 40 boys attended, and there was only one father that attended the event. I asked the boys to please be truthful and don't be ashamed to answer a question. The question was how many of them live with their real father? Out of 40 boys only three hands went up. I could see the shame on the faces of most of the other boys, I told them that they are their father's children, but they are not their father's choice; and they can make better choices in their lives.

One of my favorite books says," The glory of the children is their fathers" this should be a true saying. Webster defines glory as something that," secures praise or renown." Where is praise and renown that children should have for their fathers? Where are the fathers that these children, especially boys can look up to? Fathers were important in the lives of their children from the beginning of time, and they are equally important now. Fathers are needed to fill a void in the lives of children and specifically that of a boy. A father's influence can push a boy to the top or bring him down to the bottom.

If that father is absent, inaccessible, distant or abusive, the boy has only a vague notion of what manhood is all about. Fathers hold the keys to manhood and they must influence the boy's life in a positive way. R.J. Miller said it well," there have been meetings of only a moment which have left impressions for life, for eternity. No one can understand that mysterious thing we call influence. Yet, every one of us continually exerts influence to heal, to bless or leave marks of beauty, to wound, to hurt, to poison or to stain other lives."

Sociologists tell us that the most introverted individual will influence 10,000 other people during his or her lifetime. Fathers hold the power to lead their boy to success, failure, gangs, or drugs. Helen Keller was asked," What would have been worse than being born blind? She replied," To have sight without vision." Sadly, too many of our boys have sight without vision. They have a mental picture of what a man should be, but they have no one to substantiate their personal claim to manhood.

A father can add vision to his son's sight, thus bringing into focus a sharper and clearer image of what manhood entails. Where are the fathers that will reveal their true selves, so that the boys may know their own identity? Son, such a small word – but it gives way of being a part of someone greater than yourself. To hold life in your hands and cast it aside is atrocious, but to embrace it, love it, and give it direction is paramount. I heard a little story about an eagle.

This big eagle was flying high in the sky and saw a sight he couldn't believe, so he went down for a closer look. He saw a baby eagle in the barn yard with a group of chickens. As he swooped down over the barnyard all the chickens began to run, but as the baby eagle ran he tripped over his very large wings and fell right in front of the big eagle. The big eagle said," what are you doing down here pecking around like a chicken? The baby eagle said," But I am a chicken, I live in a chicken coop, I eat chicken food, they call me chicken, and I come."

The big eagle said," You are not a chicken, you are an eagle; but you've got your head in the dirt eating anything. Eagles don't eat just anything. Why, you didn't even see me coming. But I could see you from over 1000 feet in the air because I have what is called eagle vision. I have such visual acuity that I could see you from that height. You are not a chicken, you are an eagle. You are the one that fell out of the nest and was raised by chickens. You are not a chicken, you are an eagle. You just forgot your identity.

Many of our boys have forgotten their identity. A father gives identity, vision, and direction. A father has the courage to tell his son that he is not a chicken, but he is an eagle. Our boys face emotional and psychological struggles without fathers in their lives. The crucial need in the lives of these boys is not affirmative action, programs, or welfare. The crucial need is the attention of the fathers. Our boys don't need another motto to say, they need a model to see. Are you raising chickens or eagles?

Without knowledge the people perish

WHEN I WAS A CHILD I remember sitting at my grandparent's feet, they would tell the children stories of days gone by. We were told about the good times, the bad times, the struggles, and the times when they had nothing but the clothes on their back. But they made it through, and they didn't have to beg, borrow, or steal. They worked, and they worked hard to earn every penny they had. I remember my parents getting up early in the morning before the sun came up, preparing to go to work.

I watched my father as my mother prepared his breakfasts, as he prepared for a long day at work. I knew as a child that I would have to fulfill that same role one day, because I was taught that one day I would have a family, and it would be my responsibility as a man to take care of my family. That knowledge was passed on to me, from my parents and from my grandparents. I knew I would have to be a man one day, because it was expected of me.

No one told me that this was what I had to do, but I knew through the knowledge that I was given at the feet of my grandparents and through my parents; that I would have to pass this knowledge on to my children and their children one day. But as I look at the youth today I ask myself, where is the knowledge that should have been passed on from the parents and grandparents? Where is the work ethic that should be demonstrated by the youth of today?

Out of respect for my parents and my grandparents, I would have never dreamed of raising my voice or talking back to my parents or grandparents. I was taught to respect authority, grown-ups, and my elders. I was taught to treat women with respect, and not to say or do anything that would cause shame to my family. Where is the knowledge that should have been passed down from grandparents and parents to the youth of today?

Knowledge that was meant to keep them on the right path of dignity and respect for themselves and others. Our youth are lost, because there is a lack of knowledge, a lack of discipline, a lack of respect, and more importantly; a lack of role models to pass that knowledge down to the next generation. Because we have lost our way, our youth has no clear path to follow. The Bible says in 2nd Chronicles 7:14 (NKJV), "My people are destroyed for lack of knowledge. Because you have rejected knowledge, I also will reject you from being priests for me; because you have forgotten the law of your God, I will also forget your children".

Here are just a few examples of the situations and circumstances that our youth face every day. Let's start in our own backyard, a study commissioned by the Kenosha YMCA indicates that the impact of poverty - such as homelessness, lack of food and clothing, poor healthcare, limited access to transportation, depression, and language barriers - is one of the most difficult problems faced by youth growing up in the Frank Neighborhood (Rabic Marketing, 2011).

Here's another situation our youth face, as reported by Kate Murphy and Jordan Rubio from News21. At least 28,000 children and teens were killed by guns over an 11-year period. For every

US soldier killed in Afghanistan during 11 years of war, at least 13 children were shot and killed in America. More than 450 kids did not make it to kindergarten. Another 2700 or more were killed by a firearm before they could sit behind the wheel of a car.

Every day, on average, seven children were shot dead. We as a country tolerate violence when it is in low income black communities, because we come to accept that the acceptable face of gun death is black, we allow it to continue to happen. There is an epidemic of violence that is pervading our neighborhood and communities. It will only stop when we as a community stand up to our worst enemy, and that is ourselves. When will we began to take back our streets, our schools, our children, our homes, and our dignity?

If we would look in the mirror we will see the problem, we are the problem because we have allowed ourselves and our children to lose sight of the knowledge, purpose, strength and resolute, that was passed down from generation to generation of strong African-Americans people. Dennis Prager asked the question; is America still making men? My answer is no, America never did make men. Fathers shaped and molded boys into men. I agree with what Dennis Prager said," when boys who are not transformed into men they remain boys, and when too many boys do not grow up into men, women and society suffers."

What is a man (as opposed to a boy)? Dennis Prager said," the traditional understanding was that a man is he who takes responsibility for others, for his family, his community, his country, and, of course, for himself. He goes on to say," I knew what a man was supposed to be, and I knew that society, not to mention my parents, expected me to be one."

When I acted immaturely, I was told to act like a man. I wonder how many boys are told to "be a man" today; and if they were, would they have a clue as to what that meant? Many families and society seem to have forgotten boys need to be made into men. Without knowledge the people perish, our youth need men that will lead them back to the path of dignity and respect for themselves and others.

Frederick Douglass said; "it's easier to build strong children, then to fix broken men." Come on people, let's build strong children. I read a poem called Unity, Sculpting young minds. (Author unknown). I dreamed I stood in a studio and watched two sculptures there, the clay they used was a young child's mind and they fashioned it with care. One a parent with a guiding hand and a gentle loving heart, one a teacher - the tools he used were books and music and art.

Day after day the teacher toiled with a touch that was deft and sure, while the parent labored by his side and polished and smoothed it over. When at last their task was done they were proud of what they had wrought. For the things they had molded into the child, could neither be sold or bought. Each agreed he would have failed, if he had worked along. For behind the parent stood the school and behind the teacher stood the home. Come on people, we have the knowledge, and it's our responsibility to pass it on to our children. Pass it on.

Words have the power
of death and life

WHEN I WAS A CHILD in Mississippi my stepfather said something to me that I will never forget, he said that I would never amount to anything. That statement stayed in the back of my mind all throughout my teen years. Even into my adult years those words rang out in my mind. I believed what he said about me to be true because he was the adult and I was the immature child. I don't think he even knew the power that was in the words that he spoke to me that day, had he known I don't believe he would've said them. I had no idea that words could be so powerful and life altering, words can destroy a life, or they can build up a life.

Proverbs 18:21 (NKJV) says," Death and life is in the power of the tongue." We as a nation of believers so easily forget how powerful the spoken word is. In the book of Genesis chapter 1 reads," In the beginning God created the heavens and the earth. Verse 2 reads." The earth was without form, and void; and darkness was on the face of the deep. And the spirit of God was hovering over the face of the waters. Verse 3 reads." Then God said.' Let there be light"; and there was light. Verses 3 – 6 – 9 – 11 – 14 – 20 – 24 – 29 says," And God said. His words created something out of nothing, by his authority he spoke it and it was so.

Proverbs 18:21(NKJV) says," Death and life is in the power of the tongue." You have been given creative power through your words, and for that reason we must be careful when speaking negative words to ourselves or others. People can voice their opinion about you and make you think it's true, but it's not what they say about you, it's what you believe about yourself. I believed what my stepfather said about me because I was a child, and I looked up to him as the voice of authority in my life. After I grew up and learned my identity about myself and what I had been given, I began to understand just how powerful words were.

Words can alter your concept of yourself, which alters your life and causes you to live a life of fulfillment or a life of doubt, fear, and purposelessness. At the school and in the neighborhood where I work I see young people and adults that are living beneath their potential, because they don't know their identity or what they are capable of. I believe God gave us enlighten teachers to set us on a path of discovery that would uncover hidden treasures within ourselves to change our lives and those around us. Our first teacher should be our parents. They are the gatekeepers that God has charged with the duty of speaking the words of life that will build a strong foundation upon which their children will stand.

Proverb 18:21 (NKJV) says," Death and life are in the power of the tongue, and those who love it will eat its fruit. Nelson Mandela, who opposed the South African apartheid regime and was imprisoned for almost 3 decades, knew the power of words. He is often quoted today, but while in prison his words could not be quoted for fear of repercussion. A decade after his release he said: "It is never my custom to use words lightly." If 27 years in prison have done anything to us, it was to use the silence of solitude to make us understand how precious words are, and how real speech is in its impact on the way people live and die."

King Solomon, author of most of the Old Testament book of Proverbs, wrote often about the power of words. He said, "Death and life are in the power of the tongue" Prov. 18:21(NKJV). Words have the potential to produce positive or negative consequences (v. 20). They have the power to give life through encouragement and honesty or to crush and kill through lies and gossip. How can we be assured of producing good words that have a positive outcome?

The only way is by diligently guarding our hearts: "Above all else, guard your heart, for everything you do flows from it" (4:23 NKJV). Jesus can transform our hearts so that our words can truly be their best—honest, calm, appropriate, and suitable for the situation. Let the words of my mouth and the meditation of my heart be acceptable in Your sight, O Lord, my strength and my Redeemer. We must learn to guard our heart in everything that we say, so that we might be encouragers and not discouragers. Is there someone that your words have destroyed? Now is a good time to speak words that will edify that person that you have hurt. Be the change that you want to see in others. Until next time, be encouraged.

You have a Purpose, you are Salt and Light

I WAS TOLD YOU CAN lead a horse to water, but you can't make him drink. I have found that not to be true, if you put salt in his oats I guarantee he will drink. I see the same principle at work in so many people live, you lead them to resources that can change their lives and they do nothing with it. Tools and techniques that will enable them to live empowered and productive lives, you lead them to the well of life and they refused to dip their buckets.

I'm reminded of a story of a ship that was stranded at sea, for almost a week they were stranded without drinking water. the captain sent out an SOS that said," help in need of drinking water," for days the ship drifted with no help in sight. Finally, a ship was spotted on the horizon, and as the captain sent out another SOS that said," help in need of water," and everyone saw the ship getting closer, and suddenly it turned and went the other way.

The captain and crew were devastated, but the other ship signaled back and said dip your buckets. It seemed like such a cruel thing to say to someone dying of thirst, but one crew member more desperate then the others decided to try it. When he drew up the bucket and tasted the water it was fresh, the stranded ship had drifted into the current of the mighty Amazon River that accounts for up to 1/5 of the earth fresh water supply.

They had been sitting in freshwater for days, but they were dying from thirst. So many families, men, women, and children have the necessary resources all around them, but they refused to dip their buckets into the resources that are all around them. On my radio show, last week my guest was Debbie Rueber from the Division of health, who runs a program called Prevent Suicide Kenosha County. She reported that since 2000 we have lost 357 people to suicide in Kenosha County, and in 2015 we have already lost 16 people to suicide.

Just like the ship stranded in a sea of freshwater but dying of thirst. I was so encouraged today by several young men that were so positive, respectful, and courteous. I was at the YMCA talking to another gentleman, and these two young men were listening very intently at our conversation as we spoke about things that were and things that are going on in society today. Our conversation was seasoned with salt and these two young men were thirsty to hear what we had to say.

How many of us are making our conversations worth hearing? How many of us are seasoning our conversations with wisdom, truth, and integrity? You can lead a horse to water, but you can make him drink. If his oats are seasoned with salt, he will be thirsty. There is help for the poor, there is help for the homeless, there is help for those that have lost their way, there is help for those that are thinking about taking their lives.

But we must remember what my favorite books says", you are the salt of the earth; but if the salt loses its flavor, how shall it be seasoned? It is then good for nothing but to be thrown out and trampled underfoot by men. You are the light of the world. A city that is set on hill cannot be hidden. Nor do they light a lamp and put it under a basket, but on the lampstand, and it gives light to all who were in the house.

There is someone in your house right now that need the light that you must shine in their lives. There is someone that needs your conversation to be seasoned with salt and love. Let's not hide our love, let's began to show it that others might feel it and know how important they are. Finally, let your light shine before men, that they may see your good works and glorify your father in heaven. Your light was meant to shine, that others may see it and have the same hope that you have.

Although things look bad, we still must have hope. Everyone needs to hope, we must keep hope alive and show others how to keep hope alive. When you talk, is your conversation season with the salt? Can someone look into your eyes and see the light of life? Or do they see darkness and fear? Do they see a glimmer of hope? Or do they see hopelessness? You are salt, you are light, you were meant to be a blessing to someone, someone's life is on hold today until you speak life into their life, are you ready to be salt and light for someone? Be encouraged my friends and know that you have a purpose, you are salt and light.

Out of the mouth of a child

I WOKE UP THE OTHER morning and I was filled with so much anxiety, and all I could do was lay in my bed and stare at the ceiling. I began to pray and for some reason I picked up my phone, and I saw that the very same person that I was thinking about had sent me a link to a video. I was curious to see what it was pertaining to, so I decided to click on it. As I clicked on the link, I saw a picture of this little boy. So, I opened up the link, and what I saw and heard changed my anxiety into rejoicing. This little boy was so handsome in his little suit and tie, he looked to be about four or five years old.

He could hardly pronounce the words of the verses that he was quoting, but they had such clarity that stirred my very soul. There was an adult reciting the alphabets to him, and for each letter of the alphabet this little boy would say a verse from the Bible that begun with that letter of the alphabet. He started with the letter A, and without fail he would give a Bible verse for every letter of the alphabet. Suddenly, my mind left my problems and began to focus on this little boy and the words that was coming out of his mouth. For all 26 letters of the alphabet he gave a Bible verse that penetrated my soul and brought joy back into my heart.

One letter and verse stood out more than all the others, it was like he was speaking directly to me and my situation. When he got to the letter R, he said," rejoice, in the Lord always, again I say, rejoice." I knew it was the hand of God, because I felt the anxiety complex shattered to pieces as soon as the word of God was spoken over it. Let me explain, have you ever saw a building being torn down by a giant crane, with a wrecking ball attached to the chain? When the giant wrecking ball smashes into the building, it is demolished, the same affect happened when the words of that Bible verse met my anxiety. The Bible verse that the little boy spoke, was like a wrecking ball to my anxiety.

It demolished all my worries, doubts, and fears. I immediately got up from my bed, went into the living room, got my Bible and started praying and praising the Lord for that little boy and my friend that sent the link to the video. I looked up the Bible verse, and I began to read it and think about it as I applied it to my life and my situation. The verse that the little boy quoted is found in Philippians 4:4 (NKJV) and it says," rejoice, in the Lord always, again I say, rejoice." As I began to read even further, verse six and seven brought everything into perspective. Which said," be anxious for nothing, but in everything by prayer and supplication, with thanksgiving, let your requests be made known to God; and the peace of God, which surpasses all understanding, will guard your hearts and minds through Christ Jesus.

Verse six said," be anxious for nothing, but in everything by prayer and supplication, with thanksgiving, let your requests be made known to God. Through prayer, supplication, and thanksgiving, we are to make our requests known unto God. Sometimes we try to solve our own problems, and that causes even more problems. The Bible tells us," to seek first the kingdom of God and his righteousness, and all these other things shall be added unto you. When we come to God and ask him for the answers, and how we should handle the situations, He shows us what to do to get the victory, and He will get the glory for it all.

As I laid on my bed that night I began to pray, and God led me to pick up my phone which had the link that had the little boy quoting Bible verses using the alphabet. Out of the mouth of a little child, using the alphabets to quote God's word to shatter the anxiety that was devouring my peace. Isaiah 11:6 (NKJV) says," the wolf also shall dwell with the lamb, the leopard shall lie down with the young goat, the calf and the young lion and the fatling together; and a little child shall lead them." This little boy led me out of my anxiety complex with God's word, and the peace of God that passes all understanding, guarded my heart and mind through Christ Jesus.

Christians do not have to live in a state of anxiety, worry, fear, and confusion. In fact, being anxious and afraid is sin. The secret of overcoming anxiety is to rejoice constantly in the Lord and pray to God, thanking him for his provision, his goodness, and his mercy, both past and future. When you know that your heavenly father is taking care of your business, you can allow the peace of God to fill your life. God's peace is not dependent on outward circumstances. It is supernatural peace that comes from the confidence of knowing that God is in control. Be encouraged my friends, pray and seek the Lord, and he will send the answer to your problems and anxieties also.

About the Author

W.M. Harris grew up in Mississippi on a plantation with his mother and stepfather, who were sharecroppers. he spent his teenage years in Chicago where he was involved in gangs, drugs, and violence, After a shooting incident and breaking his mother's heart, she made the a decision that changed her son's life forever. Little did he know, that through his mother's decision to dedicate him to the Lord, his life was now on a collision course with destiny. His every decision was now stepping stones that led him to God's purpose for his life. The very unclear choices that he made, would later be used to show God's power to shape the path of his life. God heard a mother's prayers, and those prayers moved the hand of God throughout W.M. life.